Paul Gayler with

Jacqui Lynas BSc RD

# healthy eating for
# your heart

Photography by Peter Cassidy

Kyle Cathie Limited

# contents

## dedication

To Anita and family 'Home is where the heart is.' **(PG)**

To my husband, Jonathan, for his love, encouragement and help, and my dear children
Lottie, Sam and Tom for their continuing patience – with much love and thanks. **(JEM)**

This edition published in Great Britain 2009 by
Kyle Cathie Limited
122 Arlington Road
London NW1 7HP
general.enquiries@kyle-cathie.com
www.kylecathie.com

First published 2003 by Kyle Cathie Limited

ISBN 978 1 85626 874 5

Text © 2003 Paul Gayler and Jacqui Morrell
Photography © 2003 Peter Cassidy
Book design © 2003 Kyle Cathie Limited

Senior Editor Muna Reyal
Designer Carl Hodson
Photographer Peter Cassidy
Home economist Linda Tubby
Styling Penny Markham
Copy editor Anne Newman
Recipe analysis Dr Wendy Doyle
Production Sha Huxtable
A Cataloguing In Publication record for this title is available from the British Library.
Colour reproduction by Sang Choy
Printed and bound in Singapore by Star Standard

## important note

The information and advice contained in this book are intended as a general guide to healthy
eating and are not specific to individuals or their particular circumstances. This book is not
intended to replace treatment by a qualified practitioner. Neither the authors nor the
publishers can be held responsible for claims arising from the inappropriate use of any dietary
regime. Do not attempt self-diagnosis or self-treatment for serious or long-term conditions
without consulting a medical professional or qualified practitioner.

# foreword by H·E·A·R·T UK

Books that are written with you, the cook, in mind, are a joy to read and use – here is one such publication that fits that bill perfectly. At the same time, it helps to address the concerns that we should all have about eating with health in mind because it reaches the parts that we at HEART UK most certainly endorse.

Much of our time as a charity is spent being concerned about those who need to eat healthily – it is to those people, many of them with inherited high cholesterol, that we suggest it is their 'first change for the better'.

More than 100,000 in the UK inherit high levels of cholesterol. They have familial hypercholesterolaemia, known as FH, and they have to be particularly careful about what they eat. For most, drug therapy will be part of their daily lives. With our help, advice and counselling they have discovered that dull and boring food need not be on their menus.

Although for them strict diet and drug therapy are necessary, millions of others have an inherited predisposition to high cholesterol. So, it is equally important that we all benefit from a change for the better; and what better way than diving into these pages and reinventing the best of food for your table, your family and their better heart health?

Much of what you, the cook and reader, can do to help reduce the risk of heart disease in your family is described here between the covers of this book – without compromising the looks and taste of your food. Here particularly, the result is at the opposite end of the spectrum: variety, spice and excitement are included in all the ingredients and thus the repast!

Pleasurable page upon pleasurable page – and each leaf turned is utterly good for you! Enjoy yourselves and enjoy your food!

If you would like to know more about the work of H·E·A·R·T UK, please contact the charity by post, telephone, email or visit our website: 7 North Road, Maidenhead, Berkshire SL6 1PE  Tel: 0845 450 5988  Email: ask@heartuk.org.uk  Website www.heartuk.org.uk

# introduction

Cardiovascular disease (CVD) is the number one killer in the world with 12 million deaths each year, a figure that is increasing annually. CVD is a collective term which includes not only coronary heart disease (CHD), but also stroke and all other diseases of the heart and circulation. It causes 35 per cent of deaths in the UK, killing around 200,000 people. About half of the deaths from CVD in the UK are from CHD and more than a quarter from stroke. Although the death rate from heart disease in the UK is falling, it still remains one of the highest in the world, claiming one victim every six minutes. It is a disease that affects men and women, accounting for one in five deaths in men and one in seven deaths in women. It kills three times more women than breast cancer.

## Long-term effects

These alarming statistics are only part of the story, as heart disease is also a major cause of ill health which can be debilitating, affecting a sufferer's quality of life significantly. In the UK, approximately 2 million people suffer from angina, 700,000 from heart failure and there are 146,000 heart attacks per year, of which about 30 per cent are immediately fatal. For those lucky enough to survive a heart attack, life is never quite the same again.

Heart disease has developed into a common lethal epidemic and we are all likely to know someone – a member of the family, a friend, or colleague – who has been touched by this disease. The tragedy is further compounded when heart disease and heart attacks are premature, cheating the victim of either a healthy quality of life or their natural life expectancy.

## Changing your life

On a brighter note, the good news is that heart disease is potentially avoidable and preventable. Most of the risk factors for heart disease can be reduced by following a healthy lifestyle. In essence, this means not smoking, doing plenty of physical activity, maintaining a sensible weight and choosing a healthy diet. Even if you already have heart disease it is never too late to change your ways and the onset of symptoms is a particularly good time for you to reassess your lifestyle.

### Heart food

A healthy diet can have a positive influence on the majority of risk factors for heart disease including cholesterol levels, blood pressure, weight and diabetes. It is estimated that at least 30 per cent of deaths from heart disease are due to unhealthy diet. Using sound scientific research as well as consensus opinion, nutritional experts have identified several inter-related, multi-faceted strategies for eating for a healthy heart. Latest advice highlights the overall benefits of a varied diet which, whilst low in fat, has the right balance of different fats, includes an abundance of plant foods and is low in salt. However, the effects of diet are very complex and although there have been some remarkable discoveries in recent years, there is still much to explore.

The emerging picture is that to try to protect against heart disease we should adopt a dietary pattern similar to that traditionally eaten in Mediterranean and Asian countries. The key to good heart protection is to eat fresh foods: plenty of fruit, vegetables and salads, fish, whole grains, beans, nuts and seeds, together with moderate amounts of lean meat and low-fat dairy foods. These dietary recommendations are in line with others which help people to enjoy healthy eating for the prevention of cancer, diabetes and obesity.

# about heart disease

Heart disease or, more specifically, coronary heart disease is caused by a hardening or narrowing of the arteries which surround the heart. These blood vessels supply fuel and oxygen to the heart muscle, allowing it to pump blood to all the organs in the body. Ageing, poor diet and an unhealthy lifestyle cause fatty, cholesterol-laden deposits to form in the smooth artery linings, a process which can even begin in childhood.

## Angina

Angina is often the first sign of heart disease, signalled by pain across the chest but sometimes in the shoulders, arms, throat or jaw. The narrowed coronary arteries reduce the rate at which blood can be delivered to the beating heart muscle. The pain is usually a heavy or tight one, generally lasting for under 10 minutes. Angina commonly occurs with strenuous activity, as this makes the heart beat faster and increases its need for energy and oxygen. The discomfort of angina occurs more readily in cold, windy weather, after eating a large meal or with excitement or stress. Rest, relaxation and, for some, using angina medication usually bring relief in a few minutes. The situation becomes more serious when angina occurs at rest or with minimal activity or comes on with increasing frequency or severity.

## Heart attack

A heart attack occurs suddenly when a blood clot forms in a narrowed coronary artery, completely blocking blood flow and thereby causing an area of the heart muscle to die. Commonly, the pain is severe and crushing, lasting for longer than 15 minutes and not relieved by rest. The outcome depends on the site and size of the artery involved and the affected area of the heart muscle. When only a small area is involved, there is a good chance of a full recovery. However, if larger areas are involved, the heart attack may prove fatal or result in an incomplete recovery as the heart muscle loses some of its power and strength. Sometimes the heart will stop altogether or abnormal heart-beat rhythms (arrhythmias) take over and both of these scenarios can cause sudden death.

## Stroke

Most incidences of stroke occur in a similar way to heart attacks, but the arteries concerned are those that supply the brain. Stroke occurs when part of the brain has been deprived of blood flow, usually because of a sudden blockage in the artery caused by a blood clot. 'Mini-strokes' can occur when the brain is briefly deprived of its blood supply but manages to recover within minutes. People who have had heart attacks are at increased risk of stroke and vice versa.

**Classic Risk Factors for Coronary Heart Disease**

Some you cannot change:
* Age – the older you are, the greater the risk
* Male sex – women are at lower risk before the menopause
* Family history – especially heart disease in a close relative under 55 years old (man) or 65 years old (woman)
* Ethnicity (eg. being South Asian)

Some that can be reduced, controlled or eliminated:
* High blood cholesterol
* High blood pressure
* Diabetes
* Being overweight
* Smoking
* Lack of physical activity

# reducing risks

## Cholesterol

This is a soft white waxy substance that is essential to health as it is a building block for all cell membranes, bile salts, vitamin D and various hormones. Cholesterol is only a problem if you have too much of it as this can increase your risk of heart disease. Cholesterol comes from two sources. The majority is made in the body, mostly in the liver from saturated fat, but it is also found in foods that are obtained from animals, such as fatty meats, poultry, fish, seafood, eggs and dairy products.

A 1 per cent reduction in blood cholesterol can translate into a 1–2 per cent lower risk of heart disease.

### 'Good' and 'bad' cholesterol

Cholesterol is transported in the bloodstream in tiny 'carriers' called lipoproteins. The types of carrier are classified by their density, the two most important carriers being low-density lipoprotein (LDL) and high-density lipoprotein (HDL). Most of the blood cholesterol is carried from the liver to the body's tissues in low-density lipoproteins and is therefore called low-density lipoprotein cholesterol or LDL cholesterol. A high level of this increases your risk of heart disease. This is because, in modified forms, it can slowly build up in the walls of coronary arteries, forming 'atherosclerotic plaques', the fatty deposits that narrow the arteries and ultimately cause angina and heart attacks. To simplify matters, LDL cholesterol is often called 'bad' cholesterol, and the lower it is, the better.

Conversely, cholesterol carried in high-density lipoproteins is called HDL cholesterol. HDL cholesterol is thought of as 'good' cholesterol, as high levels reduce the risk of heart disease and low levels increase the risk of heart disease. HDL cholesterol seems to act as a 'biological hoover,' removing cholesterol from the body cells, including artery walls, and returning it to the liver for excretion. The higher your HDL cholesterol, the lower will be your risk of heart disease.

### Triglycerides

Triglycerides are the most common form of fat both in the diet and in the human body and are often stored subcutaneously just where we don't want them! Most of the triglycerides, a different kind of fat from cholesterol, are carried in very low density lipoprotein (VLDL). These particles also contain small amounts of cholesterol which can be deposited in the wall of the artery, increasing the risk of heart disease. Very high levels of triglycerides can cause pancreatitis. High blood triglyceride levels are often seen in people who are overweight, have Type 2 diabetes or drink too much alcohol. Research has shown that even if your cholesterol level is normal, if you have a high level of triglycerides and a low level of HDL cholesterol, you may still be at increased risk of heart disease. Keeping fit, slim and enjoying a healthy diet which includes oily fish or fish oil keeps triglyceride levels under control.

### What are lipids?

Lipids are the collective name for fatty substances in the blood. If you want to know your levels you will need to have a blood test. A fasting blood test (where you fast for 12–16 hours, drinking only water) will tell you the level of both LDL and HDL cholesterol as well as your level of triglycerides. A random, non-fasting test measures just the total and HDL cholesterol.

### What is a good lipid pattern?

The average cholesterol level of most people in the UK is around 5.4 mmol/L (211mg/dL) yet in areas of rural China the average cholesterol level is 3.0mmol/L (115mg/dL) and the rate of heart disease in those places is very low. It is likely that the lower the cholesterol level, the better. If you can keep your cholesterol level low enough, there is a good chance that any atheroma, which has already been deposited, will stabilise or even regress.

If you already have heart disease or are at high risk of developing it, your doctor may have prescribed medication to modify your lipid levels. The benefits of these drugs are significant and their effect is enhanced by a healthy diet.

### Reasonable targets to aim for are:

* Total cholesterol level below 5.0mmol/L (195mg/dL)
* LDL cholesterol level below 3.0mmol/L (115mg/dL)
* HDL cholesterol above 1.0mmol/L (39mg/dL)
* Triglyceride level below 1.7mmol/L (151mg/dL)

(If you have had a heart attack or stroke or have diabetes or are at high risk of CVD then lower targets are set for total cholesterol (below 4.0mmol/L (156mg/dL)) and LDL cholesterol (below 2.0mmol/L (78mg/dL))

# High blood pressure

Everybody has – and needs – blood pressure. A certain amount of blood pressure is vital to keep blood flowing through the arteries, delivering energy and oxygen to all parts of the body. Blood pressure is only harmful if it becomes too high, usually as a result of the arteries losing their elasticity. As the heart beats, blood is pumped into the arteries and a pressure is created, which causes blood to circulate through the body. When your blood pressure is measured two numbers are recorded, for example 120/60 mmHg (millimetres of mercury). The top number (systolic pressure) measures the pressure in your arteries when the heart beats. The bottom number (diastolic pressure) measures the pressure whilst your heart rests between beats.

There is much discussion about what constitutes 'normal' blood pressure, but the table below shows the most recent recommendations (high normal is the highest 'normal' value before it becomes abnormal).

Your blood pressure can change from minute to minute because of changes in posture, exercise, during sleep and particularly when you are anxious, and therefore several readings should be taken over a period of time, before a decision is made about blood pressure.

Normal blood pressure should be less than 140/90 mmHg. If you have heart disease, it should be less than 140/85 mmHg and even lower if you have diabetes or kidney disease because of the higher risk of heart disease associated with these conditions.

If your blood pressure constantly measures above 140/90 mmHg, you have high blood pressure or hypertension. This adds to the workload of your heart and arteries. The heart must therefore work harder than normal and this may cause it to enlarge. As you grow older your arteries will harden and become less elastic and high blood pressure speeds up this process. High blood pressure can be controlled by a combination of healthy eating, physical activity and medication. A cardio-protective dietary pattern, avoiding salt, reducing alcohol and keeping slim have all been shown to reduce blood pressure.

## Diabetes

Diabetes is on the increase worldwide; around 2.3 million people have been diagnosed with diabetes in the UK and it is estimated that more than 500,000 people have the condition but do not know it. Type 1 diabetes develops when the body produces little or no insulin and is treated by insulin injections and a healthy balanced diet. Type 2 is the most common type of diabetes and develops when the body can still make its own insulin, but not enough for its needs, or when the insulin that the body does make is not used properly. It is treated by a healthy diet or a healthy diet and tablets and sometimes insulin injections. Type 2 is linked to obesity, especially when there is excess weight around the stomach; as obesity increases worldwide, so does the time bomb of Type 2 diabetes. Alarmingly, the fuse has been lit even in the younger generation who are developing Type 2 diabetes in their teens because they are overweight, as a result of a poor diet and also a lack of physical activity.

People with diabetes have up to five times increased risk of CVD. Reducing risk factors is therefore particularly important for people with diabetes.

**Blood pressure recommendations**

|  | Systolic blood pressure mmHg | Diastolic blood pressure mmHg |
|---|---|---|
| Optimal | Less than 120 | Less than 80 |
| Normal | Less than 130 | Less than 85 |
| High normal | 130–139 | 85–89 |

## Maintaining a good weight

Obesity rates have trebled in the past twenty years, and if current trends continue, 9 out of 10 adults and two-thirds of children will be overweight or obese by 2050. Obesity is related to other risk factors for heart disease – higher blood pressure, higher blood cholesterol levels and increased risk of Type 2 diabetes. The good news is that even modest weight loss (5–10 per cent of initial weight) is linked to significant health benefits.

**Are you apple- or pear-shaped?**
It is not just being overweight that is the problem, but where the weight is deposited. There is an association between body shape and heart disease, such that people who are 'pear-shaped', with fat deposited over their hips and thighs, seem to be at much lower risk than those who are 'apple-shaped' with fat carried around the front, like a 'pot' or 'beer' belly. Fat cells deposited over the abdomen make the body more insulin resistant, resulting in a classic clustering of risk factors, called the insulin-resistance syndrome. More insulin is produced, which increases the tendency to diabetes, increases blood pressure, cholesterol and triglycerides, lowers HDL cholesterol and increases the tendency for the blood to form clots. Health professionals are increasingly using waist measurement rather than weight to identify people at risk of heart disease. Check your own shape by measuring your waist with a tape measure (midway

**Waist measurements**

| | Aim for | Increased risk – your health could suffer. Don't put on more weight. | Substantial risk – your health is at risk. Seek advice on losing weight. |
|---|---|---|---|
| Women | Less than 80cm | More than 80cm | More than 88 cm |
| Men | Less than 94cm | More than 94cm | More than 102cm |
| Asian men | Less than 90cm | More than 90cm | |

between the lowest ribs and top of the hip-bone – for many people this will be around the naval or tummy button).

## Smoking

Smoking is a major cause of heart disease. People who smoke cigarettes have twice the risk of developing heart disease as those who do not. Smoking causes around a 25,000 deaths from cardiovascular disease each year. It has been calculated that each cigarette smoked reduces your life by 11 minutes. The good news is that stopping smoking carries an almost immediate benefit and the risks of smoking reduce progressively after stopping. If you smoke, you should get help to quit! Even passive smoking increases the risk of heart disease by 25 per cent. Smoking also increases the risk of cancer and lung disease.

## Lack of physical activity

Many people take no physical activity during a typical week. Physical inactivity roughly doubles the risk of heart disease and is a major risk factor for stroke. Accumulating evidence suggests that regular activity such as brisk walking, cycling, dancing or gardening are useful for the prevention and treatment of heart disease, stroke, diabetes, obesity and osteoporosis. Recent research also suggests that even everyday movement results in other benefits including cushioning the effects of stress, alleviating and preventing depression, reducing levels of anxiety and improving self-esteem. It is recommended that you should walk, cycle or swim for 30 minutes on at least five days of the week and if you don't have 30 minutes to spare, try to do 15 minutes twice or 10 minutes three times a day. Such activities should leave you feeling warm and slightly out of breath.

Take it slowly at first; there is no need to exhaust yourself. Walking is a great exercise to start with as it provides all the exercise your heart needs and you can build it up gradually, increasing the distance and pace little by little.

# the cardioprotective diet

In the 1960s, Dr Ancel Keys, an American epidemiologist, and his colleagues examined the relationship between diet and heart disease rates in seven countries and found that people who lived along the Mediterranean Sea suffered only a tiny fraction of the heart attacks and coronary deaths experienced by Americans and people in Western industrialised countries. The dietary fat consumed by Mediterranean people was mostly of vegetable origin in contrast to diets rich in highly saturated animal fats from meat and dairy products consumed in other countries.

The population of Crete has the lowest rate of death from heart disease and the longest life expectancy of all the Mediterranean countries. A Cretan diet is rich in legumes, fruits, vegetables, olive oil and red wine. The diet is also high in alpha-linolenic acid (see page 16) from wild plants, legumes, walnuts, figs and snails and much lower in linoleic acid (see page 16) than other Mediterranean diets. Interestingly, in terms of the essential fatty acid and antioxidant content (see page 22), the diet of Crete is similar to the Palaeolithic diet with which humans evolved over tens of thousands of years ago.

The term 'Mediterranean diet' was coined in the cookbook *How to Eat Well and Stay Well, the Mediterranean*

**What are the characteristics of a cardioprotective diet?**

* Low in saturated fat

* High in monounsaturate (mainly olive oil)

* Rich in omega-6 and omega-3 polyunsaturates

* Plenty of fruits and vegetables; rich in cardioprotective nutrients

* High in wholegrain cereals, vegetables and legumes

* Moderate amounts of lean meat, fish, dairy foods and eggs

*Way* written by Ancel and Margaret Keys in the late 1950s, promoting the delicious foods that happen to protect against heart disease and several common cancers.

The Mediterranean diet has now come to epitomise the cardioprotective diet. Other cultures have evolved diets of similar nutritional composition and they also have low rates of heart disease. The cuisines of many Asian countries provide such examples and experts have coined the phrase the 'Mediterrasian' diet.

# Fats in the cardioprotective diet

Some fat is important in the diet as it is a provider of concentrated energy, an energy store and necessary for thermal insulation. Fat is also a vehicle for the fat-soluble vitamins A, D, E, and K and the 'essential' fats, linoleic and alpha-linolenic acid, which cannot be made in the body. However, we eat too much fat, particularly saturated, which raises blood cholesterol and leads to heart disease. Recommended fat intakes are based on energy needs and physical activity levels. Present guidelines suggest that no more than 30–35 per cent of daily energy intake should come from fat and no more than 10 per cent from saturated fat. The energy needs for an average woman and man are 2000 and 2500 kcals per day respectively (see table above).

In addition, some fats are more beneficial than others. There are three main types

**Energy requirements**

| Energy Intake in Calories | Total fat in grams | Saturated fat in grams |
|---|---|---|
| 2000 | 73 | 22 |
| 2500 | 92 | 28 |

(Explanation of calculations: the percentage of energy derived from fat is 33 per cent of 2500, i.e. 825 kcals. There are 9 kcals in each gram of fat, so this equates to 825÷9 = 92g of fat).

of fat in food – saturated, monounsaturated and polyunsaturated. All fatty foods are made up from a mixture of the three but are classified according to the type of fat present in the largest amount. Saturated fats are found mostly in animal products and most are solid at room temperature; palm oil and coconut oil are non-animal and non-solid saturated fats. Monounsaturated fats are found in olive and rapeseed oils and in spreads made from them. Polyunsaturated fats, often liquid at room temperature, are found in vegetable oils, such as sunflower, safflower, and in spreads made from them, as well as cereals, nuts and seeds.

**Saturated fat**
Foods high in saturated fat are found mainly in meat and dairy produce and are the major influence on the level of cholesterol in the blood. Cholesterol is made in the liver and the amount produced is directly related to the amount of saturated fat in the diet. The more saturated fat we eat, the higher our blood cholesterol. On the other hand, foods which contain cholesterol have very little influence on blood cholesterol,

even cholesterol-rich foods such as egg yolks, liver, sweetbreads, prawns and shellfish. This is because these foods contain relatively little saturated fat, and not all of the cholesterol is absorbed anyway. This means that the most important thing to look out for is the saturated fat content.

Trans fats are found in certain foods in small amounts and behave much like saturated fats. They are found naturally in small amounts in meat and dairy products but they are also formed when vegetable oils are hydrogenated to make solid fats for processed foods such as cakes, biscuits, pastries and fast foods.

**Monounsaturated fat**
When monounsaturated fat is used in place of saturated fat, blood cholesterol levels are lowered. Olive oil, a basic constituent of the Mediterranean diet, is rich in monounsaturates. In addition it is rich in antioxidants (see page 22) and contains a substance called squalene which has anti-inflammatory properties, slows blood clot formation and lowers cholesterol. Another good

| | Main sources | Effect on risk factors |
|---|---|---|
| Saturated fats | Fatty meats and meat products, lard, dripping, suet, dairy products such as whole milk, cream, butter and cheese. Coconut oil, palm kernel oil and palm oil used in convenience foods, cakes, biscuits, etc. | Raise cholesterol |
| Trans fats | Found in small amounts in the fat of dairy products and some meats but mainly in hydrogenated vegetable oils and in prepared foods such as biscuits, etc. | Raise cholesterol |

monounsaturated oil to use is rapeseed oil (canola), which is the oil used for most vegetable oils (always check the label).

Monounsaturated fatty acids are particularly beneficial as their chemical nature makes them resistant to oxidative changes. Olive oil has remarkable stability and can be stored for eighteen months and more. This resistance to the development of rancidity is combined with a marvellous variety of flavours and colours, allowing for a range of culinary applications with little or no processing. A simple traditional salad dressing can be created instantly by combining olive oil and fresh lemon juice, which creates a rich source of both lipid-soluble and water-soluble vitamins.

In salads or in cooking, olive oil is usually mixed with herbs and spices, which are also important elements of the cardio-protective diet. Herbs like oregano, rosemary and thyme are rich sources of phenolic compounds with strong antioxidant activity. These herbs maintain the nutritional value of the food and enhance the shelf life of the product.

### Polyunsaturated Fats – Omega-6 and Omega-3

There are two main families of polyunsaturated fatty acids: the omega-6 family, which are derived from the essential fatty acid linoleic acid, and the omega-3 family derived from the essential fatty acid, alpha-linolenic acid. Omega-6 are found mainly in seed oils and polyunsaturated spreads. Omega-3 are found in oily fish (marine sources) and in some seed oils and vegetables (plant sources).

Both omega-6 and omega-3 reduce the risk of heart attacks but have different and important biological effects. Omega-6 lower blood cholesterol levels whilst marine omega-3 reduce the risk of blood clots and inflammation and also prevent abnormal heart rhythms. Marine omega-3 may also exert a beneficial effect on blood pressure and lower blood triglyceride levels. Both omega-6 and omega-3 are important 'good' fats and

| | Main sources | Effect on risk factors |
|---|---|---|
| Monounsaturated fats | Olive oil, rapeseed oil (canola), peanut or groundnut oil, nuts and nut spreads, avocados | Lower cholesterol when used instead of saturated fat |

many of us could eat more for optimal heart health. Most of us do not eat enough omega-3s, possibly because high amounts of omega-3 are found in relatively few foods. Oily fish is the richest source of the long-chain omega-3 fatty acids – eicosapentanoic acid (EPA) and docosahexanoic acid (DHA).

## Fish

One of the most extraordinary nutrition revelations in recent years has been the role of fish in preventing heart disease. Studies have shown that eating fish can avert potentially fatal disruption of heart rhythms and reduce the thickness and stickiness of the blood, which in turn means less chance of a blood clot and the start of a heart attack. There is a lower incidence of heart attacks among people who eat fish regularly, such as the Japanese and Greenland Inuits, than among non-fish eaters. The Food Standards Agency advises eating two servings of fish per week, one of which should be oil-rich (see table on page 18). It is recommended that people who have already suffered a heart attack eat two to three medium servings of oil-rich fish per week or take a daily fish oil supplement of 1g EPA and DHA. For vegetarians DHA produced by algae can be bought as a supplement.

|  | Main sources | Effect on risk factors |
| --- | --- | --- |
| **Omega-6** | Vegetable oils such as sunflower, safflower, soya, corn oil and spreads | Lowers blood cholesterol |
| **Omega-3 plant sources** | Flaxseeds and oil (linseed) rapeseed (canola), soya oil, walnut oil and walnuts, green leafy vegetables | Lowers blood cholesterol |
| **Omega-3 marine sources** | Oily fish | Reduces thrombosis, inflammation and fatal arrhythmias. May reduce blood pressure and triglycerides |

| Oil-rich fish which are high in omega-3 fatty acids (EPA and DHA) | |
| --- | --- |
| | Omega-3 (grams per average portion) |
| Mackerel | 4.5 |
| Kipper | 3.7 |
| Fresh tuna | 3.0 |
| Trout | 2.9 |
| Kipper (tinned) | 2.7 |
| Salmon | 2.5 |
| Herring (pickled) | 2.2 |
| Pilchards (tinned in brine or tomato sauce) | 1.8 |
| Salmon (pink or red, tinned) | 1.4 |
| Smoked salmon | 1.3 |
| Mackerel (tinned in sauce or oil) | 1.3 |
| Sardines (tinned) | 1.2 |
| Swordfish | 1.1 |
| Tuna (tinned in oil) | 0.7 |
| Crab (tinned in brine) | 0.6 |
| Cod | 0.3 |
| Tuna (tinned in brine) | 0.1 |

The amount of omega-3 in fish varies according to the seasons, and whether fish is wild or farmed.

### Plant sources of omega-3

Alpha-linolenic acid, the plant source of omega-3 is found in some seed oils, for example, linseed, rapeseed and soya, and in some nuts (particularly walnuts) and green leafy vegetables. The body can synthesise longer-chain EPA and DHA from alpha-linolenic acid but the conversion rate is slow. Therefore it is important to eat both fish and plant sources of omega-3 to increase the amount of omega-3 in our diet.

| Plant sources of omega-3 fatty acids (alpha-linolenic acid) | Omega-3 (grams per average portion) |
|---|---|
| Flaxseed and flaxseed oil (linseeds and linseed oil) | 1.8 |
| Walnuts | 1.5 |
| Walnut oil | 1.3 |
| Rapeseed oil | 1.0 |
| Soya oil | 0.8 |
| Vegetable oil, blended | 0.7 |
| Soya margarine | 0.2 |
| Baked beans | 0.2 |
| Spinach and leafy green vegetables of all kinds | 0.2 |
| Peanuts | 0.2 |
| Corn oil | 0.1 |
| Olive oil | 0.08 |
| Bread rolls (white or wholemeal) | 0.08 |
| Almonds | 0.04 |
| Sweet potatoes | 0.04 |
| Green peppers | 0.02 |

| Other sources of omega-3 fatty acids | Omega-3 (grams per average portion) |
|---|---|
| Chicken, dark meat, roasted | 0.33 |
| Roast leg of lamb | 0.24 |
| Cheddar cheese | 0.19 |
| Whole milk | 0.15 |
| Chicken, light meat | 0.13 |
| Grilled bacon | 0.12 |
| Roast leg of pork | 0.11 |
| Roast beef | 0.10 |
| Boiled egg | 0.06 |
| Yogurt | 0.01 |

Some chickens fed on a special diet produce eggs which contain 0.5g of omega-3 per egg. Meat and dairy products can contain a useful source of alpha-linolenic acid, especially if the animals are grass-fed.

**Key action points**

✱ The secret of low-fat cuisine is to replace some of the added fats and oils in your cooking with aromatic vegetables, herbs and spices which will provide fresher and more vibrant flavours. Try tomatoes, black olives, chillies, pepper, tinned beans, aubergines, mushrooms, herbs and spices such as ginger, garlic, fresh coriander, roasted cumin, coriander seeds, vinegar and citrus juices.

✱ Oils may be used in tiny amounts but every tablespoon contains 120 kcals, so cut down the amount you use as much as possible, especially if you need to watch your weight.

✱ The healthiest spread for bread is probably a drizzle of extra virgin olive oil.

✱ Butter contains too much saturated fat and there is a vast array of spreads and margarines to confuse you. Choose a spread with a low saturated fat content less than 15g of saturated fat per 100g.

✱ Avoid spreads with hydrogenated vegetable oils as these are as bad as saturated fats; spreads made from monounsaturated and polyunsaturated oils such as olive oil, sunflower or soya oil are good choices.

✱ If you are trying to lose weight choose a low-fat spread that contains 38g of total fat or less per 100g.

✱ Spreads with added plant stanols and sterols (see page 26) are also effective in reducing LDL cholesterol levels by about 10 per cent.

# Fruit and vegetables in the cardioprotective diet

The World Health Organisation and other health bodies have recognised the importance of a diet containing fruit and vegetables. Epidemiological studies have repeatedly shown that populations whose diets include plenty of fruits and vegetables have lower rates of heart disease and cancer than those which don't. The UK recommendation is for at least five portions (400g) of fruit and vegetables a day where fresh, frozen, dried and tinned all count. On average, people in the UK eat only three portions a day and the National Diet and Nutrition Survey of 4–18-year-olds, published in 2000, found that one in five children ate no fruit.

| What counts as a portion? | |
| --- | --- |
| Apple, orange or banana | 1 fruit |
| Very large fruit, e.g. melon, pineapple | 1 large slice |
| Small fruit, e.g. plums, kiwis, satsumas | 2 fruit |
| Raspberries, strawberries, grapes | 1 cup |
| Fresh fruit salad, stewed or tinned fruit | 2–3 tablespoons |
| Dried fruit | ½–1 tablespoon |
| Fruit juice | 1 glass (150ml) |
| Vegetables, raw, cooked, frozen. or tinned | 2 tablespoons |
| Salad | 1 dessert bowl |

1 portion of fruit or vegetables is roughly the size of your clenched fist.

Although potatoes are a vegetable they count as a starchy carbohydrate and not as a portion of fruit and vegetables.

| Antioxidants | Good sources |
| --- | --- |
| Vitamin E | Nuts, wheat germ, vegetable oils (namely seed oils), margarine, eggs |
| Beta-carotene | Highly coloured fruits and vegetables such as carrots, broccoli, tomatoes, red peppers and pumpkins |
| Lycopene (a carotenoid) | Tomatoes |
| Vitamin C | Citrus fruits and green leafy vegetables customarily eaten raw in Mediterranean countries, so avoiding loss of vitamin C produced by cooking |

| Antioxidant trace elements | Good sources |
| --- | --- |
| Selenium | Beans and lentils, Brazil nuts, oily fish, sesame seeds, soya, walnuts |
| Zinc | Almonds, berries, broccoli, hazelnuts, mangoes, pine nuts, pumpkin, sesame and sunflower seeds, soya and tofu, sweet potatoes, tomatoes |

## Antioxidants

Fruit and vegetables are rich in anti-oxidants, which work to maintain health and protect us from damage caused by free radicals, which can injure cells and tissues. The body produces free radicals in the normal course of energy production, but certain pollutants (chemicals, smoke, solar radiation) trigger the production of free radicals. LDL cholesterol is vulnerable to oxidation by free-radical attack and oxidised LDL cholesterol is much more toxic and likely to accumulate in the artery wall.

Antioxidants include vitamin E, vitamin C, beta-carotene, selenium and zinc. In addition, some non-nutrient substances have been shown to have strong antioxidant properties, and may play a protective role. These include polyphenols (found in wine, tea and olive oil), organic sulphides (in garlic) and anthocyanins, responsible for the fabulous colours in fruits and vegetables.

## Non-vitamin antioxidants

Trace elements and polyphenols are powerful antioxidants and are particularly abundant in the Mediterranean diet because of the high proportion of fruit and vegetables consumed.

Selenium is of particular interest because the main source of selenium in the UK diet is wheat and hence bread. Since joining the European Market, the UK has imported its wheat from Europe rather than the United States. The wheat from Europe has a lower selenium content than that from the US because of soil conditions and therefore it is important to seek out good sources of selenium in the diet. Three Brazil nuts a day would provide sufficient intake.

In the Mediterranean basin, as a result of the warm climate and the prolonged exposure of crops to sunlight radiation, some plant species such as olives, grapes and dark-coloured leaves are particularly abundant in polyphenolic compounds. Polyphenols have applications in folk medicine as antibiotic, anti-diarrhoeal, anti-ulcer and anti-inflammatory agents. Several other diseases, for example, hypertension, have been successfully treated with plant extracts particularly rich in polyphenols. Researchers have identified more than 5,000 flavonoids (a form of polyphenol) in plants, some in fruits, beans, roots and leaves that are eaten as a food or used to make drinks. They are found in considerable quantities in fruit, fruit juices, vegetables, grains, tea, cocoa, red wine and soya.

## Chocolate

Scientists have known about the antioxidant activity of polyphenols in chocolate for over fifty years. These are responsible for the excellent keeping qualities of chocolate and for preventing the dairy fats from becoming rancid. There is a growing body of evidence that cocoa flavonoids have cardiovascular health benefits, not only due to their antioxidant effects on LDL cholesterol, but also because of their aspirin-like effects on platelet function, their ability to relax the linings of arteries, their beneficial effects on immune function and their anti-inflammatory role. The quantity of natural flavonoids in chocolate depends on the variety of cocoa bean, the growing conditions, processing and storage. Unfortunately, chocolate also comes with saturated fat, sugar and calories and therefore should be enjoyed only occasionally!

## Wine

In France, the incidence of heart disease is remarkably low, despite a diet rich in saturated fat and the presence of other risk factors (such as smoking and high cholesterol levels). This apparent contradiction has been termed 'the french paradox' and has been attributed to the possibility that the French custom of drinking wine with meals may provide protection against heart disease.

The protective effects of moderate wine consumption are possibly due to the alcohol-induced increase in high-density lipoprotein (HDL) levels and to the effects of the small amounts of polyphenols found in wine.

| 1 unit (10ml) of alcohol is: |
| --- |
| 1 small beer, lager or cider (300ml) |
| 1 small glass of red or white wine (125ml) |
| 1 single measure of spirits (25ml) |
| 1 small glass of fortified wine, e.g. sherry, vermouth (50ml) |

Alcohol is, however, a dependency-inducing toxin and drinking above sensible limits is a danger to health. It also supplies extra calories (around 100 kcals per unit) which do not help if you have a weight problem. The Department of Health's current 'sensible' daily limits suggest no more than 2–3 units (see table above) for women and 3–4 units for men. It is both the pattern of drinking and the amount that are important rather than the type of drink. Avoid binge drinking and keep to safe levels of alcohol with some alcohol-free days.

## Key action points

* Keep to sensible drinking limits (see above) and quench thirst with water.

* Alternate alcoholic with non-alcoholic drinks.

* Drink at least 1.5 litres (6–8 glasses) of fluid each day, which can include tea, coffee, water, fruit juice, soft drinks, etc. (However, no more than six mugs of coffee are recommended because of the caffeine content.)

## Olive oil

Olive oil is the principal source of fat in the Mediterranean diet. The flavour of extra virgin olive oil complements raw vegetables which are generally dressed with olive oil and vinegar (the latter also contains antioxidants). Unlike other oils, olive oil contains phenolic compounds, which provide its unique aroma and taste and have been shown to exert potent beneficial actions. Most vegetable oils are extracted from seeds by solvents, whereas olive oil is obtained from the whole fruit by means of physical pressure, without the use of chemicals. The phenolic fraction in extra virgin olive oil is significantly higher than in plain olive oil.

## Antioxidant supplements

Recent clinical trials have confirmed that there seems little benefit in taking individual nutrients such as vitamins E, C or beta-carotene in supplement form. The advantages may occur only when the antioxidants are part of a cardio-protective diet in which the abundance of bioactive compounds provided by fruit, vegetables, wine and olive oil work together to benefit your heart.

## Folic acid

Fruit and vegetables also supply other protective nutrients such as folic acid. A diet with an adequate supply of folic acid, B6 and B12 vitamins helps to reduce the levels of homocysteine in the blood. Homocysteine is produced naturally in the body when protein is metabolised. High homocysteine levels have been associated with heart disease as high levels are toxic and can damage artery walls. Since 1998, the US Food and Drug Administration (FDA) has stipulated that enriched grain products, including breakfast cereals, be fortified with folic acid, although there has been, to date, no such legislation in the UK.

### Good sources of folic acid:

* liver
* yeast extract
* green leafy vegetables
* pulses
* oranges

Foods that have been fortified with folic acid, particularly breakfast cereals, are now widely available and can increase significantly total intake.

## Legumes

Legumes, such as beans, peas and pulses are good sources of the cholesterol-lowering soluble fibre and are full of cardioprotective nutrients such as arginine, vitamin E, the B vitamins, folic acid and minerals such as calcium, iron and zinc. Vegetarians have been shown to have less risk of heart disease compared to non-vegetarians and this is both because of their diet and also other healthy aspects of their lifestyles. Beans, peas and pulses are low in fat and high in protein and can be used instead of, or combined with, meat or fish. There is a great variety of beans to choose from: chickpeas, borlotti beans, lentils, black-eyed beans, peas and sweetcorn. They can be bought dried, then soaked and cooked in plenty of boiling water (usually for an hour) until soft. Lentils take a much shorter time to cook. Kidney beans release a toxic substance whilst they are being cooked, but as long as they are boiled rapidly for at least 10 minutes at the beginning of the cooking time, this substance is destroyed completely. There is also a great selection of tinned beans which are just as nutritious and available in most stores.

## Soya beans

Soya beans are worth a separate mention as there is emerging evidence that increasing the amount of soya protein in the diet has health benefits for heart disease, cancer, women's health and osteoporosis. Studies have shown that an intake of 25g per day of soya protein can reduce LDL cholesterol by about 6 per cent. In the USA and UK a health claim has been approved for soya which states that '25g of soya protein a day as part of a diet low in saturated fat and cholesterol may reduce the risk of heart disease.'

It may be difficult to obtain 25g of soya protein per day, but some substitution of meat and dairy products is certainly possible. The soya bean contains some fat which is mainly polyunsaturated fat containing the essential fatty acids, linoleic and alpha-linolenic acid. Soya beans are a particularly useful source of the plant form of omega-3. In addition to these nutrients, soya beans contain a wealth of phytochemicals. One potent group of phytochemicals called isoflavones is virtually unique to soya. Isoflavones are phytoestrogens with weak oestrogenic effects and Asian populations that regularly eat soya foods have a lower incidence of hormone-dependent cancers – breast, colon and prostate cancers.

Traditional soya foods include soya beans, miso, soya milk, soya oil, soya margarine, soya nuts, soya sauce, tempeh, tofu and tofu products. New-generation soya products include concentrated forms of food ingredients such as soya protein isolate, soya protein concentrate, soya flour and textured soya protein. Soya protein is typically consumed in the UK as soya milk, yogurts, desserts, tofu, mince and vegetarian sausages and in a wide variety of bread and bakery products, e.g. cereal bars.

## Nuts

Nuts are an important part of the cardio-protective diet. Recent studies suggest that frequent nut consumption may be protective against heart disease because of the beneficial effects on blood lipids. In clinical studies, diets supplemented with walnuts or almonds decreased levels of LDL cholesterol and total cholesterol. Other valuable constituents include high amounts of vegetable protein, magnesium, copper, vitamin E, folic acid, fibre, potassium and alpha-linolenic acid (principally in walnuts). Although nuts are high in fat, the fat is mostly unsaturated, which has positive effects on blood lipids. Most nuts are rich in arginine, the precursor of nitric oxide, which is important for the maintenance of a healthy lining in the arteries. Coconut is the exception and contains a lot of saturated fat, particularly coconut cream, although coconut milk is lower in fat.

## Seeds

Seeds are a valuable source of protein and essential fatty acids. Linseed (or flaxseed), sesame, pumpkin and sunflower seeds are rich sources of omega-3, whilst sesame and sunflower seeds also contain omega-6. All of these seeds are packed with a wealth of vitamins and minerals such as vitamins A, B, D, E and K and folic acid, as well as the minerals calcium, iron, magnesium, selenium and zinc.

## Plant sterols and stanols

Plant sterols are natural substances, the plant equivalents of cholesterol, and are found in small amounts in vegetable oils, such as sunflower oil, rapeseed oil, soya bean oil, and in cereals, nuts and some vegetables. Stanols are largely derived from tall oil, a by-product of the pine industry. It has been known since the 1950s that sterols and stanols reduce the absorption of cholesterol in the body during digestion but only recently have satisfactory methods for extracting, concentrating and adding them to various foods, such as spreads, soft cheese, yogurt and cereal bars, been developed. Plant sterols and stanols lower cholesterol in the blood by reducing the absorption of cholesterol from the intestine. Clinical trials have shown that 2–2.5g of plant sterols or stanols, taken daily, lower LDL cholesterol by about 10 per cent.

## Portfolio Eating Plan

This is a new dietary approach to lowering cholesterol, which combines foods enriched with plant sterols, nuts (almonds), foods containing soluble fibre (oats, beans, pulses and fruits) and soya.

Evidence from clinical trials shows that following this diet plan can lower LDL cholesterol by as much as 29 per cent.

## Key action points

✳ Try to eat a wide variety of fruit and vegetables. They can be fresh, frozen or tinned. Fruit juice counts, but only for one portion a day.

✳ Make the most of the enormous variety of beans, peas and pulses by infusing them with the flavours of olive oil and vegetables such as onions, garlic, tomatoes, aubergines and herbs.

✳ Try using soya milk, soya yogurts and desserts, traditional soya protein, such as tofu or miso and textured soya protein, as low-fat, cholesterol-lowering alternatives to dairy foods and meat.

✳ Enjoy a plethora of nuts and seeds in your cereals, salads and main meals. These make truly nutritious snacks, especially when mixed with dried fruit; they are, however, a significant source of calories, so beware if you are watching your weight!

✳ Try the portfolio dietary approach – add foods enriched with plant sterols/stanols: almonds, oats, beans and pulses, and soya whenever possible to your low fat, high fibre diet.

# Wholegrain cereals, vegetables and legumes in the cardioprotective diet

People in countries bordering the Mediterranean basin tend to consume a wide variety of starchy carbohydrate foods from wholegrain cereals to vegetables and legumes. All types of bread, pasta, rice, oats, bulghur, tabbouleh, couscous, semolina, gnocchi, potatoes and other fibre-rich vegetables such as legumes are the staple foods in this region. Starchy carbohydrates lend bulk and satisfying power to your food, making it filling but not fattening, as they contain only 4 kcals per gram.

Starchy carbohydrate foods and beans, peas and pulses are the main source of fibre in the diet. Fibre is classed as both insoluble and soluble. Insoluble fibre, found in the outer layer of wholegrains and vegetables, is important for good bowel health. Soluble fibre is mainly found in beans, peas and pulses, oats, barley, rye and most fruits. It forms a gel-like mixture that slows down the digestion of foods, helping to regulate appetite and glucose levels and lower blood cholesterol levels.

Wholegrains such as wheat, corn, oats, barley, rye and rice also contain important cardioprotective nutrients including antioxidants, vitamins and trace elements, namely vitamin E, B vitamins, zinc and selenium.

Different carbohydrates affect the body in different ways and this can be gauged by their 'glycaemic index' (GI). Foods with a lower glycaemic index are better for heart health as they take longer to produce a rise in blood glucose, which ultimately improves the lipid profile by increasing HDL cholesterol.

**Particularly low GI foods are:**
* porridge, oats and high-fibre breakfast cereals

* bread with added seeds and grains, rye and pumpernickel

* pasta, noodles, basmati rice, new waxy potatoes, yams and sweet potatoes

* beans, peas and lentils

* traditional English 'stoned' fruit (apples, pears, plums, peaches)

* oranges, bananas and grapefruit

**Key action points**
* Breakfast cereals, including porridge oats and muesli, are a good way to start the day and can be eaten as a healthy snack at any time.

* Base your meals and snacks around starchy carbohydrate foods by covering half of your dinner plate with potatoes, rice or pasta and accompanying them with a delicious variety of breads.

* Choose from the wide varieties of available breads, especially those with seeds and grains; there is no need to add spread.

* Wholegrain varieties of bread, cereals, pasta and rice make healthy choices, taste better and are also more satisfying.

* The chapatti is bread at its simplest – just flour and water, with no added fat or salt.

* Potatoes eaten in their jackets or new potatoes in their skins are filling not fattening. Top baked potatoes with low-fat natural yogurt, fromage frais, flavoured cottage cheese or lower fat spreads rather than butter.

## Moderate amounts of lean meat, fish, dairy foods and eggs in the cardioprotective diet

The cardioprotective diet should contain moderate amounts of lean meat, fish, dairy foods and eggs. 'Mediterrasian' cuisine makes more use of beans, peas and pulses, either as vegetarian dishes or mixed with smaller quantities of meat or fish.

| Type of Cheese | Percentage Fat |
|---|---|
| Cottage cheese | 4 |
| Ricotta | 11 |
| Half-fat hard cheese | 15 |
| Feta | 20 |
| Mozzarella | 21 |
| Camembert | 23 |
| Edam | 25 |
| Brie | 27 |
| Soya | 27 |
| Emmental | 30 |
| Parmesan | 33 |
| Cheddar | 34 |
| Stilton | 35 |

Small amounts of dairy foods are eaten in the cardioprotective diet. Continental cheeses and feta cheese are generally lower in fat, having higher water content, while skimmed-milk products such as yogurt and fromage frais are a popular accompaniment to fresh fruit.

Although eggs contain a significant amount of dietary cholesterol in the yolk, it is the saturated fat content that actually increases blood cholesterol. There are now no recommended limits on how many eggs you should eat, but remember it is a good idea to eat as varied a diet as possible.

**Key action points**

* Eat moderate amounts of protein foods, but perhaps smaller than in the UK traditional diet. Think of the meat or fish as more of a flavour accompaniment to your main meal of starchy carbohydrates and vegetables or salad.

* If half your dinner plate is filled with starchy carbohydrates and two thirds of the other half with vegetables or salad then the final third should be for the protein part of your meal, whether fish or lean meat.

* Trim all visible fat from meat and skin from poultry.

* Choose lower-fat dairy products such as skimmed or semi-skimmed milk, lower-fat cheeses (see table, left), yogurt and fromage frais.

## Salt and sugar in the cardioprotective diet

Salt or sodium chloride has been traditionally used mainly to preserve food. However, modern preservation methods have made it redundant, yet food manufacturers continue to supply processed foods with added salt because we have become accustomed to the taste. Excessive salt consumption causes a significant rise in blood pressure, which is a major cause of stroke and heart attacks. Government recommendations are to decrease our salt intake to 6 grams per day (just one teaspoonful). Average blood pressure has fallen in countries which have launched public awareness campaigns to decrease salt intake and where potassium chloride is used in baked and processed foods.

As well as decreasing sodium, increasing potassium seems to be important in decreasing blood pressure. Potassium is found in abundant quantities in fruits and vegetables.

We are also born with a sweet tooth and while sugar intake is not directly associated with heart disease, sweet foods can add unwanted calories to the diet and can also contain saturated fat. In a cardioprotective diet, natural sweetness is provided by sumptuous fruits of all kinds, fresh, tinned and dried, all with the added bonus of providing antioxidants, vitamins and minerals such as potassium.

## Key action points

✳ Avoid adding salt to your cooking and to your food at the table. Rather enhance the natural flavours of your dishes with aromatic vegetables, herbs and spices such as garlic, onions, pepper, lemon juice, vinegar, ginger, chillies and tomatoes.

✳ Steaming and microwaving vegetables are the best ways to cook vegetables to retain all their top nutrients, flavour and taste. Serve as soon as they are cooked.

✳ Use fresh foods wherever possible and avoid processed foods. A huge amount of our salt intake (75 per cent) is already in the food we buy.

✳ Check the label for the salt content of packaged foods and choose foods which contain less than 1.5g salt (0.6g sodium) per 100g. Check for GDAs or traffic light signposting and keep to foods in the green and amber colours most of the time.

✳ If you only know how much sodium is in a food, multiply this amount by 2.5 to calculate the salt content. For example, 1g of sodium per 100g = 2.5g of salt per 100g.

✳ Try to keep your daily salt intake to below 6g (2.4g sodium).

✳ Remember: some foods that do not appear to be salty, such as bread and some cereals, can contain large quantities of salt. Check the labels.

✳ Rock salt and sea salt are still salt and should be avoided. You could use a salt substitute which contains less sodium, to wean yourself off the salt habit.

✳ Stocks and gravies can be made from salt-free, homemade ingredients, and purée vegetables such as onions, garlic, tomatoes and aubergine with a little wine to make sauces. For speed, 'diluted' stocks and gravies can be made by using half the usual quantities of stock cubes or gravy granules.

✳ Look out for vegetables, fish and beans tinned in water rather than brine or labelled 'no added salt' and choose lower-salt varieties of baked beans, bread, yeast extract, bouillon, tomato and soy sauce.

✳ Feed your sweet tooth with natural sweetness from fresh, tinned, frozen or dried fruit.

✳ Look out for low-sugar varieties of squash, fizzy drinks, jams and marmalades, jelly, baked beans, tomato sauces and fruit tinned in natural juices.

✳ Salty and sugary solutions can be removed from tinned produce by rinsing in a colander under the tap.

# a whole lifestyle approach

*Healthy Eating for Your Heart* is just one part of a complementary lifestyle approach towards better health – to help you get in shape, feel fitter and have more energy. You can make it easy for yourself by making changes gradually, rather than all at once. You'll be surprised by how even the smallest of changes can make a difference.

When it comes to eating, a balanced approach is the best – there are no good or bad foods and you can still enjoy the odd indulgence from time to time, guilt-free, provided that for the majority of time you eat:

* plenty of fruit and vegetables including legumes, nuts and seeds
* plenty of bread and other cereals (like pasta, rice) and potatoes
* moderate amounts of milk and dairy foods, low-fat where possible
* moderate amounts of lean meat and fish
* small amounts of fatty and sugary foods

Not smoking and taking plenty of physical activity are also part of this lifestyle package. If you enjoy keeping active and follow the key messages above, you will manage your weight and feel all the better for being in control.

## Weight management

The concept is easy, the practice harder! Energy taken 'in' from the food we eat each day should equal the energy we expend 'out' in the energy needs of our body and in our daily physical activity. If our 'energy in' is greater than our 'energy out', this will result in weight gain. Our energy balance is so fine that it only takes an extra biscuit each day to gain 2kg in a year! We also have to eat 3500 calories less to lose 0.5kg and that is why losing weight is so difficult. It is much better to lose weight slowly – 0.5-1kg per week – and maintain the weight loss than to do crash dieting only to regain the weight quickly, then diet again. Following the healthy lifestyle advice in this book will help you to make the changes necessary to control your weight for good, by eating a cardioprotective diet and taking more physical activity.

## Feeding the family

We all want to give our children the best possible start in life. Making the best food choices for our children helps them to form good eating habits and attitudes to food that will influence their tastes and well-being far into the future.

**Key action points**
* Get your children involved with choosing, planning and preparing meals and in shopping.
* Hands-on cooking with children encourages a love of food and cooking and can be fun too.
* Just cook one meal for the whole family which you can enjoy eating all together.
* Always serve vegetables, bread and water with your meal.
* Keep the fruit bowl well stocked with a variety of fresh produce to eat whenever you feel peckish.
* Try new foods with old favourites.

**Adapting traditional family recipes**
* Reduce the amount of fat used.
* Change the type of fat by using a monounsaturated or polyunsaturated variety.
* Cut out the salt.
* Reduce the amount of meat and add more legumes.
* Replace pastry in pies with mashed potatoes, e.g. shepherd's pie.
* Reduce the amount of sugar used; sweeten instead with dried fruit or fruit juice.
* Use yogurt or fromage frais instead of cream.
* Use half-fat cheese or smaller quantities of stronger cheeses, e.g. Parmesan.
* Grating cheese makes it go further.
* Instead of high-fat roux-based sauces, make sauces with cornflour and skimmed milk; flavour with mustard and black pepper.

Remember: forming good eating habits is just part of a lifestyle package and encouraging children to be more active and not to smoke is equally important. Living together in a pro-active environment and teaching by example is an invaluable lesson.

# A cardioprotective kitchen

A kitchen with the following equipment will encourage healthy cooking:

✳ Good-quality, heavy-based non-stick pans make low-fat cooking easier as they allow food to be cooked more efficiently without fat.

✳ Griddles and special low-fat grills allow fat to drain away from meat and meat products.

✳ Summer low-fat cooking is simple with a barbecue. Winter stews, casseroles and one-pot cooking encourage healthy infusions of cardioprotective nutrients.

✳ Microwaving and steaming food are the best ways to retain the maximum amount of nutrients.

✳ A non-stick wok is useful for low-fat stir-frying using a little oil, stock or wine.

✳ An oil-water spray allows successful low-fat frying whether you are using a frying pan, grill pan or griddle or roasting in the oven. The spray can be used directly on cooking equipment or the food itself may be given the lightest possible spray, to stop it from drying out during cooking or sticking to the pan. Oil-water sprays can be bought commercially or made up at home by combining your favourite high-quality oils (add seven parts water to one part oil). Use rapeseed oil for general purposes, olive oil for a richer flavour, walnut oil for a piquant fragrance and sesame oil for oriental dishes. Oils can be flavour-infused with your favourite herbs and spices for added zest.

## Check the labels

In the real world it is not always possible to cook from scratch and there will be times when you will need to buy pre-prepared foods or ingredients for your meal. By checking the information on a food label you will be able to make healthy choices by choosing foods which are low in fat, low in saturated fat, high in fibre and low in sugar and salt.

Ingredients are generally listed on labels in decreasing order by weight. You can also use the nutritional information and the table on page 34 to see if the product contains a lot of or a little fat, saturated fat, fibre, sugar or salt.

For ready meals and other foods eaten in large amounts as a main meal, look at the amount per serving. Check the serving size with the amount you usually eat! For snacks and other foods eaten in smaller amounts look at the 'per 100g' information. You can also use this information to compare products and choose the healthiest option.

The nutritional information on a 'ready meal' beef lasagne is shown in the table below. The suggested serving size for this lasagne is 400g and you can see that it contains 'a lot' of fat, saturated fat, sugars and salt (see the table on page 34) and would not be a healthy choice.

## Guideline daily amounts

You may also use the figures on a package to help you work out how the food fits into your whole diet for that day. The figures in the table below are based on an average-sized man or woman taking average physical activity.

## Nutritional information from a packet of beef lasagne

| Typical Composition | This pack (400g) provides | 100g provides |
|---|---|---|
| Energy | 2304kJ/548kcals | 576kJ/137kcals |
| Protein | 34.4g | 8.6g |
| Carbohydrate | 47.2g | 11.8g |
| of which sugars | 12.8g | 3.2g |
| Fat | 24.8g | 6.2g |
| of which saturates | 14.8g | 3.7g |
| Sodium | 1.6g | 0.4g |

A serving (400g) contains the equivalent of approximately 4g of salt

## Nutritional guidelines

| A lot | A little |
|---|---|
| 20g fat | 3g fat |
| 5g saturates | 1g saturates |
| 3g fibre | 0.5g fibre |
| 10g sugars | 2g sugars |
| 0.5g sodium | 0.1g sodium |
| (1.5g salt) | (0.3g salt) |

If you want to know the amount of salt (sodium chloride) in a product, multiply the sodium by 2.5.

The beef lasagne, therefore, for a man, contains about a quarter of the recommended amount of fat for the day and half the recommended amount of saturated fat. This means that your food for the rest of the day must be particularly low in fat and saturated fat to keep within healthy guidelines.

## Guideline daily amounts

| | Men | Women |
|---|---|---|
| Energy | 2500kcals | 2000kcals |
| Fat | 95g | 70g |
| Saturates | 30g | 20g |
| Fibre | 20g | 16g |
| Sugar | 120g | 90g |
| Salt | 6g | 6g |

## Claims

Choose foods that have general claims:
* healthy eating
* diet, reduced calorie or low calorie
* low fat (should have no more than 3g of fat per 100g)
* reduced fat or virtually fat free
* low salt or reduced salt
* sugar-free

but at the same time beware:
* Low-fat or fat-free does not necessarily mean low calorie or calorie-free as the food may be full of sugar and as high in calories as the standard product.
* Cholesterol-free foods may be full of fat and calories.
* Sugar-free does not mean low-calorie or low-fat; such foods may be high in both.

# Eating out

Inevitably, we can't always eat at home. In fact some of us eat 'out' almost as much as we eat at home, whether it's socially, a lunch-time sandwich, 'bites' after work or celebration meals. Healthy eating can present a challenge at these times but needn't be a nightmare. If you only go out occasionally, don't worry – just enjoy your treat! If you do eat out a lot, then you will need to use your knowledge to make healthy choices from the menu. After a while you will learn to return to the restaurant where you know that it is easy to choose the food you prefer to eat and where the food is delicious and healthy too!

## Key action points in restaurants

* Take some plain bread from the bread basket but decline the butter. Ask for extra bread and try different varieties.
* Simple starters include chilled fruit juice, melon cocktail, salads with a little olive oil dressing. Choose a vegetable-based soup with a crusty bread roll.
* Choose a baked jacket potato (no butter) with a variety of fillings. Don't forget the side salad!
* Choose plenty of vegetables or a side salad with your main course. Avoid salads with mayonnaise dressings; ask for a little olive oil, vinegar or oil-free dressing instead.
* Go for dishes which are steamed, braised, grilled, char-grilled or baked.
* Vegetarian options based around beans and pulses with pasta, rice, potatoes, bread and extra vegetables and salads make good choices.
* Water quenches both thirst and appetite, so always ask for a jug with your meal.
* For a dessert, choose fresh fruit salad or just fresh fruit. Sorbets or plain ice cream (not luxury ice cream, which contains more cream and calories) make guilt-free treats.

## In Italian restaurants

* Go for bread sticks or plain crusty bread and avoid garlic bread.
* Choose thin-crust pizza with vegetable toppings, ham, chicken, tuna, seafood and Hawaiian. These pizzas tend to be the least calorific and fatty.
* Choose pasta with tomato-based or seafood sauces, e.g. arrabbiata sauce,

napoletana, vongole, primavera, provençale, puttanesca and so on. Avoid creamy sauces.

✳ Traditional Italian dishes such as lasagne and spaghetti bolognese can be very high in fat. Some lasagnes contain more fat than a plate of fish and chips! Choose cannelloni instead, as the spinach replaces some of the fatty meat.

### In Indian restaurants
✳ Choose drier curries such as tandoori and tikka dishes.
✳ Choose saffron and plain boiled rice.
✳ Choose plain chapattis or naan breads. Ghee, the Indian cooking fat, is similar to butter in its saturated fat content.
✳ Add generous amounts of vegetables to all curry dishes. In an Indian or Pakistani home a meat curry is seldom eaten on its own.
✳ Choose tomato-based sauces like lamb rogan josh and chicken jalfrezi.
✳ Vegetable, chicken and prawn Madras are suitable and Balti or dupiaza dishes.
✳ Avoid creamy dishes such as korma, passandra and masala and oily dishes such as Bhaji, samosa or pakhora.

### In Chinese restaurants
✳ Choose soups for starters rather than battered pancake rolls.
✳ Stewed dishes, e.g. chicken with bean sprouts or pineapple, chilli prawns or crab, are good choices.
✳ Chow mein or boiled, steamed rice are good starchy bases for your meal.
✳ Stir-fried dishes are lower in fat than deep-fried dishes.
✳ Avoid deep-fried foods such as prawn crackers and sweet 'n' sour balls.

### In Thai restaurants
✳ For starters, clear soups, seafood salads and stir-fried dishes are suitable. Avoid the deep-fried options.
✳ Choose steamed or 'sticky' rice.
✳ Avoid dishes with coconut cream.

### In Mexican restaurants
✳ Good starter choices are spicy corn chowder and black bean soup.
✳ Fill up on Mexican rice and vegetable chilli.
✳ Fajitas and soft tortilla wraps are a good bet, but beware of high-fat enchiladas!
✳ Guacamole and refried beans are a mixed bag as they contain a lot of cardioprotective nutrients but are also high in fat, so take it steady!
✳ Watch out for sour cream, tortilla crisps, cheese, deep-fried tortillas!

### Fast foods
✳ In the burger bar choose a plain hamburger, cheeseburger or grilled chicken burger and order the smallest size. Share any fries and choose water, fruit juice or a diet drink.
✳ Choose a falafel sandwich or shish kebab rather than doner kebab.
✳ Opt for grilled fish from the fish and chip shop or leave the batter! Share the chips and add some vegetables e.g. baked beans or mushy peas.

### Key action points with snacks
✳ When eating sandwiches, good fillings are tuna, salmon, sardines, pilchards, roast lean meat, ham, chicken, turkey, egg, Edam, Brie, low-fat soft cheese, hummus, peanut butter and salads.
✳ Choose 'diet', 'light' and 'healthy option' sandwiches. Avoid mayonnaise and look for moist alternatives such as mustard, pickles and fromage frais.
✳ Fresh fruits and fruit salads or a handful of fresh nuts and dried fruits are good snacks.
✳ Yogurts and rice puddings – choose low-fat or 'light' varieties.
✳ Fruit buns, fruit scones, malt bread, crumpets and large pretzels make filling snacks.
✳ Ginger, Garibaldi and fig roll biscuits are good low-fat choices.

# a chef's prescription

During the early years of my training, I soon learnt that 'where there is fat, there is flavour', and if I am honest with myself, I have to agree – fat tastes good. And while there are obvious health problems associated with too much fat, simply omitting it from a dish without compensation will cause a meal to be a bland and uninteresting experience – a non-event, in fact. So the question we need to ask ourselves is how to remove the fat without sacrificing the taste.

Not so long ago, the notion of healthy eating implied denial, deprivation and boring food. But the great chefs such as Anton Mosimann in Britain and Michel Guérard in France have pioneered healthy, low-fat food, teaching us to cook without too much fat, cream and butter. With a little thought, it is actually very easy to do just this – without creating 'rabbit food'.

Let me say from the outset that this is not a faddy health cookbook. It is a book about healthy eating in today's world, using only the best-quality ingredients with imagination, flair and thought. In this book I draw on the 30 years I have spent in professional kitchens and the eclectic tastes that I have encountered while travelling the world. From these experiences I have devised over 100 recipes, presented with love and care while meeting all the nutritional guidelines. Some of the recipes are gourmet, some are more everyday in design, and there is something for every taste. This book will teach you to eat smart, heart smart, but above all, that you don't have to choose between good food and good health.

# healthy low-fat cooking methods

## Kitchen equipment
You can prepare great-tasting, healthy meals with basic cooking pans and utensils, but I would recommend that you buy a few well-made pieces that will make cooking easier and help you to obtain the most successful results:

* heavy-based non-stick frying pan
* heavy-based non-stick deep-sided frying pan suitable for oven use
* heavy-based non-stick casserole dish with lid
* non-stick roasting tin
* non-stick baking tray

## Grilling
This is an extremely healthy way to prepare food and is ideal for cooking low-fat food as you only need to spray the smallest amount of oil over your meat, fish (none is needed on oily fish) or vegetables to prevent them sticking. Use a grill rack under a conventional grill or a preheated grill pan, and remember to take advantage of the summer months by cooking on an open-grill or barbecue.

## Baking
Another low-fat cooking method. I prefer to bake small pieces of meat or fish in a non-stick baking dish. Alternatively, you can bake them in a sealed foil pouch with some fresh herbs or spices and stock. This method is very grandly known as cooking en papillote, but is very simple to do. The resultant juices, collected in the foil, can then be used to create an accompanying sauce.

## Roasting
This is not usually associated with healthy cooking as the roasting meats are usually larger in size and fattier in composition. Buy the leanest meat available. It is also better to roast small cuts of meat and seal them first in a frying pan with a very small amount of oil. If you are roasting a large piece of meat, cook it on a wire rack so that the fat drains away during cooking. A good tip is to add a few ice cubes to the baking dish; the water will help the fat solidify, which can then be removed with a spoon or kitchen paper.

## Steaming
This is perhaps the most nutritious cooking method and it requires no added fat. Instead it uses the vapour created by boiling water or stock to cook the vegetables, fish or meat that is stacked above the liquid. A simple collapsible steamer that fits snugly inside a saucepan, topped with a tight-fitting lid, is all you need for this, or you could rest a colander on top of a saucepan and cover it with foil. Chinese bamboo steamers are becoming more popular, and you can stack several layers on top of each other, which will allow you to cook more than one food at once.

## Slow-poaching and boiling
Again, these require no additional oil. Any fat released by poaching foods can be removed using kitchen paper. Poached foods are also generally easy to digest.

## Braising
This involves cooking meat, fish or vegetables in a flavoured liquid in an ovenproof dish. Generally the food is first sealed in butter or oil before being immersed in stock, but this is not essential. Dry-fry meat (or use a minimal amount of oil) in a non-stick pan until slightly coloured all over before transferring to the casserole dish. Vegetables are often added at this stage, together with any herbs or spices, and then the dish is oven-cooked (unless you have a hob-ready dish).

## Microwaving
Those of you who have read my previous books will know that I am not usually a fan of the microwave. However, through my research for this book, I have learned to be more tolerant and must admit that it does have a useful role in low-fat cooking. Microwave cooking rarely needs any fat and it is also particularly good for cooking vegetables as it needs only a small amount of liquid to cook them, thus retaining all the nutrients as well as texture and colour.

## Stir-frying

This is synonymous with Oriental food and one that we have come to enjoy. It is also a quick and nutritious way to cook using little or no oil. The ingredients cook rapidly in a wok, retaining the crunchiness of the vegetables and the juiciness of meat and fish.

## Dry-frying

This seals meat or fish in a very hot, non-stick pan without any fat and is perfect for starting casseroles or meat sauces such as the classic bolognese sauce. Dry frying browns the meat evenly and the fat leaks out of the meat as it cooks so you can drain it away easily. If you must add some fat, use an oil/water cooking spray (see page 33).

## Vapourised frying

Here chopped vegetables are sautéed in a non-stick pan or wok with a small amount of water or stock instead of oil. The liquid evaporates, coaxing the vegetables to release their natural flavours and caramelise slightly. An excellent way to exude flavour without using fat.

## PG Tips

✳ Casseroles that combine meat, vegetables and pulses or grains make tasty, filling meals.

✳ Herbs and spices produce intense flavour to compensate for the lack of fat. Dried herbs are fine to use, but their aroma and taste cannot be compared with those of fresh herbs. Ideally fresh spices should be toasted to maximise flavour before adding to dishes. Fresh herbs should be added at the last minute for most effect.

✳ Marinating meat and fish in low-fat yogurt, spices, herbs, flavoured vinegars and Asian-style sauces such as teriyaki or sweet chilli sauce will add moisture, tenderise and give flavour.

✳ Make your own low-fat stocks and sauces and freeze the leftovers for future use. You can also use the left-over liquid from cooking vegetables.

✳ When making soups, stews and casseroles, skim the fat that rises to the surface while cooking. A good idea is to make them a day ahead, then store in the fridge overnight. Any fat in the dish will rise to the surface as it cools and can easily be removed once it has solidified. This type of dish actually improves in flavour when cooked in advance.

✳ Use egg whites as a binding for stuffings or when making crumb coating as it contains no fat. As a general rule, in a recipe, replace one whole egg with two egg whites.

✳ If used for cooking purposes, low-fat spreads must contain a minimum of 40 per cent fat.

✳ Take great care when cooking with no-fat or low-fat dairy products such as yogurt and low-fat cheeses as they can curdle when boiled. Allow them to come to room temperature first, then add as required to the dish off the heat. Skimmed milk can be boiled but can separate when combined with acidic juices from lemons or tomatoes.

✳ Replace the cream in cream-based dished with skimmed milk and thicken the sauce with cornflour or flour, adding a spoonful of low-fat fromage frais before serving.

✳ One of my favourite additions to dishes is roasted garlic purée and I always keep a batch to hand. Simply place unpeeled garlic cloves in a microwave and cook for 6–8 minutes on full power until they soften. Allow to cool before popping them out of their skins and crush with a mortar and pestle, or blend to a smooth purée. Store in an airtight container.

# simple low-fat stocks

It is simple to make your own stocks and these recipes can be prepared up to 4 days ahead and stored, covered, in the fridge. Be sure to remove any fat from the surface after the cooled stock has been refrigerated overnight. If the stock is to be kept longer, it is best to freeze it in smaller quantities. Prepared stocks are also now available in supermarkets, but be aware of their salt content. Stock cubes or powder can also be used. As a guide, 1 small crumbled stock cube mixed with 600ml water will give a fairly strong stock. However, check the salt content of stock cubes and powders.

**All low-fat stocks, per 500ml:**
**14 kcals, 0.2g fat, 0g saturated fat,**
**0.65g sodium**

**Beef stock**
2kg meaty beef bones
2 medium onions, chopped
2 sticks celery, chopped
2 medium carrots, chopped
1 bay leaf
2 teaspoons black peppercorns
5 litres water

Place the bones and onions in a baking dish. Bake in a hot oven for 1 hour or until the bones and onions are well browned. Transfer the bones and onions to a large pan, then add the celery, carrots, bay leaf, peppercorns and water. Simmer uncovered for 3 hours, then strain. Makes about 2.5 litres.

**Chicken stock**
2kg chicken bones
2 medium onions, chopped
2 sticks celery, chopped
2 medium carrots, chopped
1 bay leaf
2 teaspoons black peppercorns
5 litres water

Combine all the ingredients in a large pan. Simmer, uncovered for 2 hours, then strain. Makes 2.5 litres.

**Fish stock**
1.5kg fish bones
3 litres water
1 medium onion, chopped
2 sticks celery, chopped
1 bay leaf
1 teaspoon black peppercorns

Combine all the ingredients in a large pan. Simmer, uncovered, for 20 minutes, then strain. Makes 2.5 litres.

**Vegetable stock**
1 large carrot, chopped
1 large parsnip chopped
2 medium onions, chopped
6 sticks celery, chopped
1 bay leaf
2 teaspoons black peppercorns
3 litres water

Combine all the ingredients in a large pan. Simmer uncovered for 1 hour, then strain. Makes about 1.25 litres.

# breakfasts and brunches

# fragrant fruit compôte

As a chef, I find the standard fruit compôte somewhat boring, so I decided to give my recipe a little Middle Eastern flair with the addition of some fragrant sweet spices and flavourings instead of the more traditional sugar syrup.

Juice and zest of 1 orange
1 teaspoon ground cinnamon
2 cloves
2 tablespoons orange blossom honey
50g sultanas
300g selection of ready to eat dried fruits (apricots, prunes, figs)
1 tablespoon orange flower water
Juice of ½ lemon
50g blanched almonds
30g pine kernels

**Serves 4**

**Place** the orange juice, zest, cinnamon and cloves in a pan with 150ml water and bring to the boil. Add the honey and sultanas and poach for 2–3 minutes.

**Cut** the dried fruits into bite-size pieces and add to the pan. Cook for 1 minute further, then remove from the heat. Allow to cool, then place in the fridge overnight.

**One** hour before serving, add the orange flower water and lemon juice. Leave to stand at room temperature to allow the flavours to meld together.

**Divide** the fruits into 4 serving bowls, scatter over the almonds and pine kernels and serve.

**PER SERVING:**
320 KCALS, 13G FAT, 1G SATURATED FAT, 0.03G SODIUM

# breakfast sundae

Take a few exotic fruits, vibrant with flavour and colour, and you have a refreshing breakfast sundae, which will instantly provide a good proportion of your daily fruit allowance. Almonds will also help to reduce your cholesterol levels.

1 mango, peeled and cut into 1cm chunks
1 papaya, peeled, halved and seeds removed
2 kiwi fruits, peeled and cut into 1cm chunks
1 banana, peeled and thickly sliced
125g strawberries, halved
Juice and zest of 1 orange
1 tablespoon mint, roughly chopped
4 scoops of ricotta sorbet (see page 154)
150ml low-fat natural yogurt
2 passion fruits, halved
2 tablespoons flaked almonds, toasted

**Serves 4**

**Place** all the fruits except the passion fruit in a bowl, add the orange juice, orange zest and mint and leave for 30 minutes in the fridge.

**To** serve, place a scoop of ricotta sorbet in 4 individual sundae-style glasses. Top with the fruits, then spoon over the yogurt. Scoop out the passion fruit pulp and seeds and drizzle over.

**Sprinkle** a few almonds over the yogurt and serve immediately.

**PER SERVING:**
306 KCALS, 8G FAT, 3G SATURATED FAT, 0.08G SODIUM

Crumpets are light and delicious when made with buttermilk (you could use ordinary skimmed milk if you can't get the buttermilk, or try mixing 125ml low-fat yogurt with 250ml skimmed milk).

# hot buttermilk crumpets with mixed berries

450g plain flour
Pinch of salt
600ml buttermilk
  (or skimmed milk)
15g fresh yeast
Large pinch of baking soda
4 tablespoons warm water
Oil-water spray (see page 33)
Zest of 1 lemon

**Serves 4**

Low-fat natural yogurt, to serve
  (optional)

**For the fruits**
40g caster sugar
250g mixed soft berries
  (strawberries, raspberries,
  blackberries, blueberries)
2 tablespoons honey
Juice of 1 lemon

**Place** the flour and salt in a large bowl and make a well in the centre. Heat the buttermilk until it is tepid, add the yeast and dissolve, then pour into the well.

**Use** your hands to combine the mix together into a batter. Cover with a cloth and leave in a warm place for about 1 hour until the mixture has risen. Mix the baking soda with the warm water and beat into the batter. Leave for another hour. Add the lemon zest and leave for a further 10 minutes.

**Warm** a non-stick frying pan over a low heat, then squirt with a little oil-water spray. Place some shallow metal rings or cookie cutters in the pan.

**Pour** some of the batter into the rings to about 1cm deep and cook over a low heat until a small indentation appears on the surface of the batter. Turn them over and continue cooking for a further couple of minutes. Cook 7 more crumpets in this way and keep warm.

**For** the fruits, place the sugar in a pan with 3 tablespoons water, and bring to the boil slowly. Add the fruits and cook for 1 minute, then add the honey and lemon juice and allow to cool slightly.

**Serve** the crumpets topped with the fruits, and with some low-fat yogurt if liked.

**PER SERVING:**
522 KCALS, 3G FAT, 1G SATURATED FAT, 0.47G SODIUM

# summer fruit crisp

When it comes to breakfast, I've always been able to kick-start the day on nothing more than a large cup of coffee. However, occasionally I enjoy the fresh taste of a fruity breakfast, so here is my 'breakfast crumble', ripe fruits with a crisp granola topping that really hits the spot.

2 ripe peaches
100g raspberries
1 mango
150g blueberries
150g strawberries, halved
1 tablespoon lemon juice
½ teaspoon ground cinnamon
Good-quality raspberry jam

100ml virtually fat-
  free fromage frais, to serve

**For the topping**
100g granola
30g wholemeal flour
30g brown sugar
25g low-fat spread

**Serves 4**

**Preheat** the oven to 220ºC/425ºF/gas mark 7.

**Blanch** the peaches in boiling water for 1 minute, remove with a slotted spoon and quickly refresh in cold water. Peel and halve the peaches, remove the centre stone and cut into thick slices.

**Place** all the fruits in a bowl and mix with the lemon juice and cinnamon. Arrange the fruits attractively in 4 individual oven-proof dishes.

**To** make the topping, combine all the ingredients in a bowl. Sprinkle the topping over the fruits evenly. Bake in the oven for 5–6 minutes or until the topping is golden and crispy. Remove.

**Meanwhile**, heat the jam with 2 tablespoons water until it liquefies. Drizzle over the topping and serve warm with a good dollop of fromage frais.

PER SERVING:
301 KCALS, 5G FAT, 1G SATURATED FAT, 0.16G SODIUM

# wheatgerm muesli

Mix grain, nuts and sweet poached fruits in a bowl and lace with honey for a wholesome start to the day. Wheatgerm contains vitamin B and is often used as a dietary supplement. It is widely available from health food stores.

125g organic wheatgerm
300ml apple juice
2 Granny Smith apples, peeled, cored and grated
250g low-fat natural yogurt
100g mixed nuts (almonds, cashews, hazelnuts,
  macadamias), coarsely chopped
65ml honey
2 tablespoons lemon juice
150g poached fruits (pears, apricots, prunes)

**Serves 4**

**Place** the wheatgerm in a bowl, pour over the apple juice, then cover with a cloth and leave to soak overnight at room temperature.

**The** next day, add the apples, yogurt, nuts, half the honey and the lemon juice and stir well together.

**Spoon** into 4 serving bowls, top with a selection of poached fruits, and then drizzle over the remaining honey to serve.

PER SERVING:
438 KCALS, 19G FAT, 1G SATURATED FAT, 0.06G SODIUM

# banana and cinnamon pancakes with maple-raisin syrup

A real treat for breakfast lovers everywhere, this is perfect for lazy breakfasts and late brunches. Choose soya milk instead of semi-skimmed for a really nutritious option.

150g self-raising flour
50g soft brown sugar
1½ teaspoons ground cinnamon
125ml soya milk or
  semi-skimmed milk
1 free-range egg yolk

2 free-range egg whites
4 medium bananas
100ml maple syrup
3 tablespoons raisins, soaked
  until swollen in warm water,
  then drained
2 tablespoons icing sugar

**Serves 4**

**Place** the flour in a bowl and add the sugar, cinnamon, milk and egg yolk. Whisk until thoroughly combined. Beat the egg whites until they form soft peaks, then gently fold them into the yolk mixture.

**Heat** a small non-stick frying pan or omelette pan. Pour approximately 65ml batter at a time gently into the centre of the pan and tilt the pan to ensure even coating of the base. Cook over a moderate heat until golden brown on both sides, flipping over once during the cooking. Prepare 7 more pancakes in this way and keep warm.

**Peel** the bananas and cut into thick slices. Heat the syrup and raisins in a small pan and, when boiling rapidly, add the bananas and 2 tablespoons water. Continue cooking over a high heat until the bananas are golden and caramelised; this will take about 2–3 minutes.

**Divide** the pancakes on to 4 serving plates and dust liberally with the icing sugar. Top with the caramelised bananas, and drizzle over any remaining raisin syrup to serve.

**PER SERVING:**
428 KCALS, 3G FAT, 1G SATURATED FAT, 0.19G SODIUM

# oatmeal mustard herrings

Herring is a wonderful fish – full of flavour and packed with natural goodness – yet ignored by many with the exception, perhaps, of the Scandinavians, who find terrific ways to serve it.

4 medium (120g) herrings,
  filleted
Freshly ground black pepper
1 tablespoon prepared
  English mustard
50g fresh white breadcrumbs
75g fine oatmeal
Oil-water spray (see page 33)
1 lemon, cut into wedges

**For the caper tartare**
50ml reduced-calorie
  mayonnaise
50ml low-fat natural
  yogurt
2 tablespoons superfine capers,
  rinsed and chopped
2 tablespoons flat-leaf
  parsley, roughly chopped
Squeeze of lemon juice

**Serves 4**

**Preheat** the grill to its highest setting.

**Using** a small knife, lightly score the herring fillets on each side, being careful not to score them through. Season with black pepper to taste and brush liberally with the mustard.

**Mix** the breadcrumbs and oatmeal together in a bowl, then liberally sprinkle them over the herrings, ensuring a good even coating. Turn the fillets over carefully and coat the other side well.

**Lightly** spray a baking tray with the oil-water spray. Place the herring fillets on the tray and grill for 2–3 minutes on each side.

**Meanwhile** prepare the tartare sauce. Mix the mayonnaise and yogurt in a bowl with the capers and parsley. Add the lemon juice and season to taste. Serve the grilled herrings with the lemon wedges and a good dollop of caper tartare on the side.

**PER SERVING:**
399 KCALS, 22G FAT, 4G SATURATED FAT, 0.52G SODIUM

# open-faced smoked salmon tortilla

Here the tortillas form the base of a pizza. This recipe is very tasty and the ideal way to use up any scraps of smoked salmon you may have left over. Flour tortillas freeze very well and so make ideal pizza bases at a moment's notice.

1 teaspoon unsaturated oil
1 small onion, finely chopped
400g tinned tomatoes, chopped
1 tablespoon tomato purée
2 tinned anchovy fillets, drained and finely chopped
Freshly ground black pepper
4 x 20cm soft wheat flour tortillas
400g smoked salmon, roughly chopped
2 spring onions, shredded
2 tablespoons dill, roughly chopped, plus some to garnish
25g half-fat mozzarella cheese, coarsely grated

**Serves 4**

**Preheat** the oven to 220°C/425°F/gas mark 7.

**In** a small pan, heat the oil, then add the onion and cook for 2 minutes over a moderate heat until softened. Add the tomatoes, tomato purée and anchovies and cook for 6–8 minutes or until the mixture thickens to a pulpy consistency. Season with black pepper to taste.

**Spread** the tomato mix evenly over the 4 flour tortillas, scatter over the smoked salmon followed by the spring onions and chopped dill.

**Scatter** over the mozzarella, place on a large baking tray and cook for 3–5 minutes or until the cheese has melted.

**Sprinkle** over with dill, cut each tortilla into 4 equal wedges and serve.

**PER SERVING:**
340 KCALS, 10G FAT, 2G SATURATED FAT, 2.59G SODIUM

# raspberry and orange muffins

The Americans have long had a passion for pancakes, muffins and scones; they love them at any time of the day. I've never really understood until recently how good they can be for breakfast and mid-morning snacks.

275g plain flour, sifted
1 tablespoon baking powder, sifted
110g caster sugar
1 tablespoon grated orange zest
1 large free-range egg
250ml buttermilk
4 tablespoons unsaturated oil
150g fresh or frozen raspberries

**Makes 12**

**Preheat** the oven to 200°C/400°F/gas mark 6.

**Place** the flour and baking powder in a bowl. Add the sugar and orange zest, mix well, then make a well in the centre. Mix the egg and buttermilk with the oil, then pour into the well in the flour and mix. Add the raspberries and gently fold into the mixture.

**Fill** a 12-compartment deep muffin tin with 12 paper cases. Spoon the mixture into the paper cases.

**Bake** in the oven for 25 minutes until golden brown. Allow to cool before eating them.

**PER SERVING:**
166 KCALS, 5G FAT, 0G SATURATED FAT, 0.17G SODIUM

# mango coconut porridge with palm sugar

This unusual porridge is creamy and moreish. The mango gives the sugar and coconut milk a fragrant fruity balance. For the best porridge, soak your oats in milk overnight.

200g rolled oats
400ml reduced-fat unsweetened coconut milk
40g palm sugar or brown sugar
1 mango

**Serves 4**

**Place** the oats in a bowl, add the milk and cover with clingfilm. Leave in the refrigerator overnight.

**Place** the oat mixture and 350ml water in a pan. Add the sugar and slowly bring to the boil, stirring constantly. Reduce the heat, then simmer uncovered for about 5 minutes or until the mixture thickens.

**Meanwhile**, peel the mango and cut into thick slices, discarding the stone. Serve the coconut porridge topped with the sliced mango, or top with a little low-fat yogurt mixed with fresh vanilla.

PER SERVING:
342 KCALS, 13G FAT, 8G SATURATED FAT, 0.1G SODIUM

# sofrito spanish eggs

I've always loved the rustic cuisine of Spain: no fuss, no thrills, just good hearty food packed with flavour. Spanish smoked paprika is now widely available in stores, so look out for it.

1 teaspoon olive oil
1 onion, finely chopped
1 garlic clove, crushed
50g new potatoes, cooked, peeled and cut into 1cm dice
50g cooked lean ham, cut into 1cm dice
½ teaspoon smoked paprika

400g tinned tomatoes, finely chopped
50g fresh or frozen peas, cooked
40g chorizo sausage, thinly sliced
Freshly ground black pepper
4 small free-range eggs
Oil-water spray (see page 33)

**Serves 4**

**Preheat** the oven to 170°C/325°F/gas mark 3. Heat the olive oil in a medium-sized non-stick pan. Add the onion, garlic and 2 tablespoons water, cover with a lid and sweat for 2–3 minutes until the onions are softened.

**Add** the potatoes and ham, sprinkle over the smoked paprika and cook for 1 minute to allow the smoky paprika to infuse the potatoes and ham. Add the tomatoes, raise the heat and cook until the tomatoes become thick and sauce-like in consistency, this should take about 10 minutes. Add the cooked peas and chorizo and season with black pepper to taste.

**Lightly** spray 4 cocottes or ramekin moulds with the oil-water spray, then divide the tomato mix between the moulds. Using a small spoon, make an indentation in the centre of each mould. Crack an egg carefully into the indentation. Season with black pepper.

**Place** the moulds on a baking sheet and bake in the oven for 8–10 minutes or until the whites have set, but the yolks are still liquid. Remove the dishes carefully on to individual serving plates and serve with rustic country bread.

PER SERVING:
165 KCALS, 9G FAT, 3G SATURATED FAT, 0.35G SODIUM

# 2

# soups and salads

# thai gazpacho

A play on the classic Andalusian speciality of cold vegetable soup that traditionally contains garlic, tomatoes and cucumbers. Here I've included Asian flavours. The bread is used to provide bulk, although the consistency can be as light or as thick as you like.

2 slices of white bread
400g ripe but firm tomatoes, coarsely chopped
1 onion, chopped
½ cucumber
1 green pepper, deseeded and chopped
2 garlic cloves, crushed
4 tablespoons red wine vinegar
2 lemongrass sticks, chopped
1 teaspoon red curry paste
1 kaffir lime leaf
10 Thai basil leaves, plus a few extra to garnish
150ml tomato juice
1 teaspoon caster sugar
2.5cm piece of root ginger, chopped
1 tablespoon tomato ketchup

**Serves 4**

**Soak** the bread in water for 10 minutes, then squeeze out.

**Place** the bread in a large bowl, add the remaining ingredients and stir well to combine. Leave to infuse in the refrigerator, preferably overnight.

**Remove** the lime leaf, then place in a blender and blitz to a fine purée. Strain through a coarse sieve, then return to the refrigerator until ready to serve.

**Serve** well chilled, topped with Thai basil leaves.

**PER SERVING:**
98 KCALS, 1G FAT, 0G SATURATED FAT, 0.26G SODIUM

# persian minted onion soup

A soup with the typical Middle Eastern flavours of fragrant spices and fresh mint, this is great for all seasons – perfect as a light meal in the summer or a warming, aromatic starter in winter. Choose herbs that are as fresh as possible to maximise flavour.

Oil-water spray (see page 33)
4 large onions, thinly sliced
1 teaspoon caster sugar
¼ teaspoon ground turmeric
⅛ teaspoon ground cinnamon
⅛ teaspoon ground cardamom
2 tablespoons flour
1 litre chicken stock (see page 39)
3 tablespoons lemon juice
3 tablespoons lime juice
2 tablespoons chopped mint leaves

**Serves 4**

**Heat** a squirt of oil-water spray in a heavy-based pan. Add the onions, sugar, turmeric, cinnamon and cardamom and 4 tablespoons water, cover with a lid and cook over a moderate heat for 10–15 minutes, stirring regularly until all the liquid has evaporated, leaving the onions tender, caramelised and golden in colour.

**Sprinkle** over the flour and cook over a reduced heat for 2 minutes. Gradually add the chicken stock, stirring regularly, and then bring to the boil. Reduce the heat and simmer for 40 minutes.

**Mix** together the lemon and lime juice, then add to the soup and simmer for a further 10 minutes.

**Stir** in the mint, and serve immediately.

**PER SERVING:**
107 KCALS, 1G FAT, 0G SATURATED FAT, 0.33G SODIUM

# smoked pumpkin and tortilla soup

A soup I actually created by accident, when, after a recent Halloween party for my youngest child, I came across an uncarved pumpkin. The smoked paprika gives it a warming flavour – just the job for a winter's day!

Oil-water spray (see page 33)
600g pumpkin, skin and seeds removed,
    cut into small pieces
½ tablespoon smoked paprika
1 onion, chopped
1 leek, white part only, chopped
2 garlic cloves, crushed
4 corn tortillas, broken into small pieces
850ml chicken or vegetable stock (see page 39)
100ml skimmed milk
2 tablespoons chopped flat-leaf parsley
Freshly ground black pepper

**Serves 4**

**Heat** a squirt of oil-water spray in a non-stick pan. Dust the pumpkin pieces with the smoked paprika and fry in the pan with 2 tablespoons water, covered with a lid, to colour them lightly; this should take about 10–12 minutes.

**Add** the onion, leek, garlic and tortillas, replace the lid and sweat the vegetables for a further 8–10 minutes.

**Pour** in the stock and bring to the boil, then reduce the heat to a simmer and cook for 20 minutes until the pumpkin is soft. Add the milk and stir well. Pour into a blender and blitz to a smooth purée, then return to the pan to reheat.

**Add** the parsley, season with black pepper to taste and serve.

**PER SERVING:**
221 KCALS, 5G FAT, 1G SATURATED FAT, 0.91G SODIUM

# chilled hummus, saffron and yogurt soup

A wonderful chilled summer soup with flavours redolent of the eastern Mediterranean. Hummus means chickpea in Arabic and is made by creating a paste with chickpeas and tahini.

1 teaspoon olive oil
1 onion, chopped
2 garlic cloves, crushed
1 teaspoon ground cumin
Pinch of saffron
310g dried chickpeas, soaked overnight
750ml vegetable stock (see page 39)
1 tablespoon tahini (sesame seed paste)
100ml low-fat natural yogurt
Juice of 1 lemon
2 tablespoons chopped coriander leaves
Pinch of paprika
Freshly ground black pepper

**Serves 4**

**Heat** the oil in a pan, add the onion, garlic, cumin and add 2 tablespoons water, then cover with a lid. Reduce the heat and cook for 5 minutes. Remove the lid, add the saffron and cook for 2 more minutes. Add the drained chickpeas, cover with the vegetable stock and return to the boil, then reduce the heat and cook for 40–45 minutes until the chickpeas are tender.

**Pour** into a blender, add the tahini and blitz to a smooth paste.

**Place** in a bowl and chill thoroughly. Add the yogurt, lemon juice and chopped coriander. Season with black pepper to taste and serve chilled, sprinkled with paprika.

PER SERVING:
315 KCALS, 8G FAT, 2G SATURATED FAT, 0.3G SODIUM

# chestnut and coconut milk soup with coriander

One of my favourite soups with a hint of lemon and fresh coriander. Chestnuts are usually found in stuffings, but the French use them often in soups. Vegetarians may replace the chicken stock with vegetable stock.

600ml chicken stock (see page 39)
1 garlic clove, crushed
1 onion, chopped
1 leek, white part only, chopped
2 lemongrass sticks, finely chopped
50g long-grain rice
200g tinned unsweetened chestnut purée
250ml reduced-fat unsweetened coconut milk
Juice of 1/2 lime
4 tablespoons roughly chopped coriander leaves
Freshly ground black pepper

**Serves 4**

**Place** the chicken stock in a pan with the garlic, onion, leek and lemongrass and cook for 10 minutes. Add the rice, chestnut purée and coconut milk, return to the boil, then reduce the heat and simmer for 20–25 minutes.

**Remove** from heat, add the lime juice, then pour into a blender and blitz to a smooth purée. Add a little coconut milk if necessary, strain and return to the pan to reheat.

**Finally** stir in the coriander, season with black pepper to taste and serve.

PER SERVING:
195 KCALS, 8G FAT, 6G SATURATED FAT, 0.34G SODIUM

# hot-and-sour clam broth

An oriental-inspired light soup, both delicate and interesting in flavour. Here I use clams, a favourite ingredient of mine, but you could substitute mussels or mixed seafood if preferred. Supermarkets now sell packets of cooked, mixed seafood for convenience.

1 teaspoon sugar
1 tablespoon lime juice
1 tablespoon reduced-salt
  soy sauce
750ml chicken stock (see page 39)
1 garlic clove, crushed
4 spring onions, finely shredded
75g shiitake mushrooms, sliced
2.5cm piece of root ginger, thinly shredded
75g pak choi, finely shredded
500g baby clams
½ teaspoon chilli oil
Freshly ground black pepper

**Serves 4**

**Mix** together the sugar, lime juice and soy sauce.

**In** a pan, bring the stock to the boil, add the vegetables and ginger and simmer for 8–10 minutes. Add the clams and cook for a further 2 minutes until they open. Add the sugar and juice mixture and cook for a further minute.

**Remove** from the heat, add the chilli oil, season to taste with black pepper and serve in deep bowls.

**PER SERVING:** 49 KCALS, 1G FAT, 0G SATURATED FAT, 0.48G SODIUM

# barley minestrone with pesto

An Italian-style vegetable soup that can make an impression all year round. You can vary the vegetables as you wish. The barley, which replaces the usual spaghetti or macaroni, adds a little chewiness to the soup.

75g pearl barley, soaked for 4 hours and drained
75g green cabbage, roughly chopped
1 onion, diced
1 carrot, diced
1 stick celery, diced
1 courgette, diced
4 tomatoes, deseeded, diced
1 baking potato, peeled, diced
50g frozen broad beans
1 garlic clove, crushed
1 litre chicken stock (see page 39)
Freshly ground black pepper

**For the pesto**
Handful of fresh basil leaves
2 garlic cloves, crushed

**Serves 4**

**Place** the barley in a pan, cover with cold water and bring to the boil. Cook for 25–30 minutes until tender, then drain.

**In** a large pot, combine all the vegetables with the stock and bring to the boil, then lower the heat and simmer for 15 minutes until the vegetables are just tender.

**To** make the pesto, place the basil and garlic in a blender, add 100ml of the vegetable cooking liquid and blitz to a smooth purée.

**Add** the purée to the soup, stir until combined, then add the cooked barley, season with black pepper and serve.

**PER SERVING:** 164 KCALS, 1G FAT, 0G SATURATED FAT, 0.35G SODIUM

# asopao (chicken paella soup)

This hearty soup, originating from Puerto Rico, is ideal for a one-pot meal. Traditionally the soup contains a long list of ingredients, including rice, but everybody has their own combination, handed down over the years. Serve with lots of chunky bread.

1 tablespoon unsaturated oil
1 large chicken breast, skinned and cut into fine strips
1 small onion, finely chopped
2 garlic cloves, crushed
1 teaspoon chopped oregano (or pinch of dried)
¼ teaspoon dried chilli flakes
200g tinned chopped tomatoes
75g long-grain rice
1 red pepper, deseeded and chopped
50g cooked lean ham, chopped
700ml chicken stock (see page 39)
1 tablespoon green olives, pitted and chopped
1 teaspoon superfine capers, rinsed and drained
50g cooked green peas
Freshly ground black pepper

**Serves 4**

**Heat** the oil in a non-stick pan, add the chicken strips and fry over a high heat until golden. Lower the heat, add the onion, garlic, oregano and chilli flakes and cook for 2–3 minutes. Add the tomatoes, rice, red pepper and ham.

**Pour** over the stock, bring to the boil, lower the heat and simmer for 25–30 minutes.

**Finally**, add the olives, capers and peas, adjust the seasoning with black pepper and serve.

PER SERVING: 197 KCALS, 5G FAT, 1G SATURATED FAT, 0.56G SODIUM

# prawn tamarind soup

Using the classic bisque of France as a base, I added a little tamarind to give it a slight sharpness that really works well. If using frozen tiger prawns, ensure that they are fully defrosted before use. A great soup for a dinner party.

500g fresh or frozen tiger prawns, shelled and de-veined
1 onion, chopped
1 garlic clove, crushed
1 small red chilli, deseeded and chopped
1 tablespoon tomato purée
1 tablespoon plain flour
4 tomatoes, chopped
1 tablespoon tamarind paste
2 lemongrass sticks, finely chopped
1 litre fish stock; see page 39 (or water)
1 tablespoon palm sugar (or demerara)
1 teaspoon nam pla (fish sauce)
Juice of ½ lime
Pinch of cayenne pepper
Oil-water spray (see page 33)

**Serves 4**

**Heat** a squirt of oil-water spray in a heavy-based pan. When hot, add the prawn shells and fry until red, stirring them constantly. Remove and set aside.

**Add** the onion, garlic and chilli to the pan and fry for 2–3 minutes. Stir in the tomato purée and mix well.

**Sprinkle** over the flour, mix well and cook for a further 2 minutes. Add the chopped tomatoes, tamarind paste, lemongrass and stock and bring to the boil, then reduce the heat and simmer for 30–35 minutes.

**Strain** through a fine sieve into a clean pan and add the nam pla, lime juice, palm sugar and cayenne.

**Chop** the prawns roughly into bite-sized pieces and cook in the soup for 1 minute before serving.

PER SERVING: 173 KCALS, 2G FAT, 0G SATURATED FAT, 0.67G SODIUM

# devilled caesar salad with crisp prosciutto and sundried tomatoes

Adding a little hot Tabasco or pepper sauce to the dressing gives a new twist to this classic salad that is both light and low in fat.

200g new potatoes, peeled
4 slices prosciutto (Parma ham)
Oil-water spray (see page 33)
2 thick slices wholegrain bread
1 cos lettuce, cut into pieces
2 anchovy fillets, tinned, drained, rinsed and finely chopped
100g sun-dried tomatoes (without oil)
1 tablespoon Parmesan cheese, grated

**For the dressing**
½ teaspoon Worcestershire sauce
1 teaspoon Dijon mustard
2 garlic cloves
1 tablespoon grated Parmesan cheese
125ml low-fat natural yogurt
Dash of Tabasco or hot pepper sauce

**Serves 4**

**Preheat** the grill to the highest setting.

**Place** the potatoes in a pan of boiling water and return to the boil, then cover, reduce the heat and simmer for 10–12 minutes or until just tender.

**Put** the slices of prosciutto on a baking tray, and grill until crisp, then break into fairly large pieces.

**Lightly** spray the slices of bread with the oil-water spray and toast under the grill until golden and crisp. Allow to cool, then cut into 1cm cubes.

**In** a bowl, combine the lettuce, half the anchovies, the potatoes, tomatoes and half the cheese and mix gently. Top with the prosciutto and sprinkle over the remaining cheese.

**Mix** the remaining anchovies with the dressing ingredients in a blender. Drizzle over the salad and serve.

PER SERVING:
191 KCALS, 5G FAT, 2G SATURATED FAT, 0.82G SODIUM

# chickpea, beetroot and cauliflower salad, curried egg dressing

A simple and delicious salad containing lots of texture and flavour – the curry powder gives the vegetables an added zing. Easy to prepare – it's a real winner!

12 baby beetroot with stems, washed
1 small cauliflower, separated into small florets
4 cos lettuce leaves
75g rocket leaves
400g tinned chickpeas, drained and rinsed
50g freshly picked coriander leaves

**For the dressing**
½ garlic clove, flattened with the back of a knife
1 teaspoon Dijon mustard
1 teaspoon mild curry powder
65ml reduced-calorie mayonnaise
Juice of ½ lemon
1 tablespoon half-fat crème fraîche
2 eggs, hard-boiled and chopped
Freshly ground black pepper

**Serves 4**

**Preheat** the oven to 200°C/400°F/gas mark 6.

**Place** the beetroots in a pouch of foil with 100ml water and scrunch up the foil to secure the beetroots within. Place in the oven for 40 minutes, or until tender when pierced with a small knife. Remove and leave to cool. When cool enough to handle, peel them. Cook the cauliflower florets in boiling water until just tender, but firm, refresh in cold water and drain well.

**To** make the dressing, rub the inside of a bowl with the garlic clove, and then discard it. Put in the mustard, curry powder and mayonnaise and mix well. Then add the lemon juice, 4 tablespoons water, the crème fraîche and chopped egg and season with black pepper to taste. The dressing should be thick, but still pourable.

**Place** all the leaves in a large bowl, add the beetroots, cauliflower and chickpeas and a little of the dressing. Serve on 4 plates, coating the cauliflower with a little more dressing and scattering over the coriander leaves.

PER SERVING:
52 KCALS, 11G FAT, 2G SATURATED FAT, 0.44G SODIUM

# feta-baked flatbread and chickpea salad

Flatbread is available from good Italian delicatessens; it is sometimes called *carta musica* or music sheets, as it is very thin. There are also many varieties of Middle Eastern-style flatbread which can be used.

4 sheets Sardinian flatbread, broken into large pieces
50g feta cheese, crumbled
400g tinned chickpeas, drained and rinsed
200g cherry tomatoes
20 black olives, pitted
75g flat-leaf parsley leaves
1 tablespoon pine kernels, toasted
2 bunches watercress

**For the dressing**
1 tablespoon tahini (sesame seed paste)
1 garlic clove, crushed
100ml water
65ml low-fat natural yogurt
Juice of ½ lemon
Freshly ground black pepper

**Serves 4**

**Preheat** the oven to 200°C/400°F/gas mark 6.

**Lay** the flatbread on a large baking sheet, sprinkle over the crumbled feta and bake for 2–3 minutes until the cheese begins to melt.

**In** a bowl, whisk all the ingredients for the dressing together and season with black pepper to taste.

**Place** the chickpeas, tomatoes, olives, parsley, pine kernels and watercress ingredients in another bowl, pour over the dressing and toss lightly together. Layer the salad with the flatbread and serve.

PER SERVING: 257 KCALS, 11G FAT, 3G SATURATED FAT, 0.83G SODIUM

# murgh chaat (spiced chicken and mango salad)

This is usually made with cooked chicken, but smoked chicken makes a nice alternative. *Murgh* means chicken and chaat, means to savour, and this is indeed a tempting salad, ideal for the summer months.

Juice of 2 limes
Juice of ½ lemon
1 garlic clove, crushed
2 tablespoons maple syrup
1 cooked smoked chicken, skin removed and meat shredded
2 ripe plum tomatoes, skinned, deseeded and chopped
1 green chilli, deseeded and very finely chopped
½ cucumber, deseeded and chopped
2 red onions, finely sliced
1 green pepper, deseeded and chopped
1 teaspoon cumin seeds, lightly toasted
2 tablespoons roughly chopped coriander leaves
1 tablespoon roughly chopped mint
1 mango, peeled and cut into wedges
Freshly ground black pepper

**Serves 4**

**In** a bowl whisk the juice of the limes and lemon with the garlic and maple syrup. Add the remaining ingredients and toss well together.

**Marinate** for 30 minutes before serving to allow the flavours to meld.

PER SERVING: 351 KCALS, 16G FAT, 5G SATURATED FAT, 1.44G SODIUM

# wok-seared duck salad with lemongrass and ginger dressing

I love warm salads, especially ones that have an oriental flavour. Chicken can be used instead of duck, if preferred. *Ketchap manis* is the Indonesian soy sauce, made from black soya beans.

1 teaspoon unsaturated oil
4 x 150g duck breasts, skin removed
1 tablespoon brown sugar
4 tablespoons orange juice
2 tablespoons ketchap manis
2½cm piece of fresh root ginger, peeled
1 garlic clove
12 broccoli florets
150g mixed salad leaves
1 carrot, finely shredded

75g beansprouts
Freshly ground black pepper
4 tablespoons flaked almonds, toasted

**For the dressing**
5cm piece of root ginger
100ml orange juice
2 tablespoons balsamic vinegar
2 tablespoons ketchap manis
2 lemongrass sticks, finely chopped
1 garlic clove, crushed
1 tablespoon sweet chilli sauce

**Serves 4**

**To** make the dressing, use a fine grater to grate the ginger into a bowl, then squeeze or strain through muslin so you are left with the juice only. Add the remaining ingredients and season to taste. Set aside.

**Heat** the oil in a wok, add the duck breasts and seal all over. Then add the sugar, orange juice, ketchap manis, ginger and garlic and cook for 10–12 minutes, basting regularly until the duck is cooked and glazed all over. Remove and keep warm. Cook the broccoli in boiling water.

**Place** the salad leaves, broccoli, carrot and beansprouts in a bowl, add a little dressing and toss well. Season with black pepper to taste.

**Cut** the duck into thin slices, top with salad, pour over a little dressing and serve, scattered with the toasted almonds.

**PER SERVING:**
376 KCALS, 18G FAT, 3G SATURATED FAT, 1.36G SODIUM

# spiced prawn salad (pla talay)

A salad I have prepared for numerous dinner parties, with great success. Other shellfish like lobster could be substituted if preferred. Nam pla (fish sauce) is available from major stores and oriental supermarkets.

2 tablespoons lime juice
1 tablespoon nam pla (fish sauce)
1 teaspoon sesame oil
2 tablespoons reduced-salt soy sauce
1 small red chilli, deseeded and finely chopped
½ garlic clove, crushed
1 teaspoon caster sugar
1 avocado

400g fresh or frozen large tiger prawns, cooked
2 lemongrass sticks, very finely shredded
2 shallots, thinly sliced
2 tablespoon finely shredded mint leaves
4 spring onions, halved and finely shredded lengthways
1 green papaya, peeled and finely shredded (optional)
100g watercress

**Serves 4**

**In** a bowl, mix together the lime juice, nam pla, sesame oil and soy sauce, then add the chopped chilli. Add the garlic and sugar and mix well together.

**Cut** the avocado in half lengthways, remove the stone and halve again. Carefully peel off the outer skin and cut the flesh into long, thin slices. Add the prawns and avocado to the bowl.

**Add** the remaining ingredients and carefully toss the lot together. Dress on individual plates and serve immediately.

**PER SERVING:**
215 KCALS, 9G FAT, 1G SATURATED FAT, 2.21G SODIUM

# chilled noodle seafood salad

Most supermarkets sell cooked seafood, which, I have to say, is pretty good quality and certainly takes a lot of tedious preparation work out of the dish. This is a simple but satisfying salad, perfect for the summer months.

250g tagliatelle
250g pack cooked seafood selection
4 spring onions, shredded
2 plum tomatoes, deseeded and chopped
¼ cucumber, chopped
Freshly ground black pepper
2 tablespoons roughly chopped dill

**For the dressing**
½ teaspoon Dijon mustard
½ garlic clove, crushed
Juice of 1 lemon
1 tablespoon olive oil
1 teaspoon honey

**Serves 4**

**First** make the dressing by placing the mustard and garlic in a large bowl. Add the lemon juice, olive oil and honey, whisking well to amalgamate.

**Cook** the pasta in boiling water until tender and al dente, drain well, then add to the dressing and toss thoroughly together. (Adding the pasta when hot allows it to absorb the flavours in the dressing.) Add the seafood, spring onions, tomatoes and cucumber, season with black pepper to taste and leave to cool to room temperature.

**Add** the dill and toss before serving.

**PER SERVING:**
320 KCALS, 5G FAT, 1G SATURATED FAT, 0.5 SODIUM

# smoked trout, orange and blueberry salad with rocket and tarragon

The combination of smoked fish and fruit is legendary as the fruit not only counteracts the richness of the fish, but also gives a pleasant freshness to the salad.

6 sweet navel oranges
2 tablespoons caster sugar
2 teaspoons Dijon mustard
2 teaspoons arrowroot, dissolved in 65ml cold water
2 tablespoons chopped tarragon
250g blueberries
2 tablespoons pine kernels, toasted
300g rocket leaves
400g smoked trout, skin removed and flaked

**Serves 4**

**Squeeze** the juice from 2 of the oranges. Place in a non-stick pan, add the sugar and mustard and bring to the boil. Whisk in the dissolved arrowroot, reduce the heat and stir until thickened. Allow to cool.

**Using** a small knife, peel the remaining oranges, ensuring all the white pith is removed. Quarter the oranges lengthways, then cut crossways into thick slices.

**Place** in a bowl, add the orange and arrowroot mixture, tarragon, blueberries, pine kernels and rocket leaves and toss to coat. Sprinkle over the flaked smoked trout and serve.

**PER SERVING:**
286 KCALS, 9G FAT, 1G SATURATED FAT, 0.79G SODIUM

# 3

# light meals and appetisers

# artichokes provençale

Artichokes are a fiddly vegetable to prepare, I will admit, as you have to get past their tough bracts and chokes, but once you've mastered their preparation you'll love to try cooking them in lots of different ways. This dish is also great served cold.

4 globe artichokes
2 teaspoons olive oil
100ml dry white wine
1 garlic clove, crushed
400g ripe plum tomatoes, skinned, deseeded and cut into 1cm dice

2 sprigs of thyme
Freshly ground black pepper
Pinch of sugar
16 black olives
2 tablespoons pine kernels
12 fresh basil leaves, snipped

**Serves 4**

**Cut** the artichoke stalk 2½cm below the artichoke's base. Remove the fibrous, dark green outer leaves until the tender, yellowish-green inner leaves are revealed. Cut off between one and two thirds from the top of the artichoke, leaving about 2½cm of leaves above the base. Using a small knife, trim the base and pare the remaining tough, dark green leaves to expose the tightly packed central leaves that conceal the hairy centre choke. Scoop out the raw choke with a teaspoon.

**Place** the artichokes upside down in a non-stick pan. Whisk together the olive oil, wine and 150ml water and pour over the artichokes. Bring to the boil and add the garlic, chopped tomatoes, thyme, black pepper and sugar.

**Reduce** the heat to low, cover with a lid and cook until the artichokes are all tender, this should take about 20 minutes. Remove the lid, discard the thyme, add the olives, pine kernels and basil, adjust the seasoning and serve.

**PER SERVING:**
184 KCALS, 8G FAT, 1G SATURATED FAT, 0.46G SODIUM

# grilled asparagus and leeks mimosa

Despite the implications of its name, buttermilk is much lower in fat than ordinary milk, commercially made by a similar method to that used for yogurt. It has a slightly sour taste that makes it more interesting than plain skimmed milk.

400g asparagus, trimmed
200g baby leeks
Freshly ground black pepper
2 teaspoons olive oil

**Serves 4**

**For the mimosa dressing**
1 tablespoon white wine vinegar
1 teaspoon Dijon mustard
2 tablespoons chopped tarragon
3 tablespoons buttermilk
1 teaspoon caster sugar
2 eggs, hard-boiled and chopped
2 tablespoons olive oil

**To** make the dressing, whisk together the vinegar and mustard in a bowl. Add the tarragon, buttermilk, sugar and eggs and blend in the oil.

**In** separate pans, blanch the asparagus and leeks in boiling water for 2 minutes, then remove and drain. Place in a shallow dish and season with black pepper. Pour over the olive oil, toss and leave to cool.

**Heat** a ridged grill pan until very hot, add the leeks and asparagus and cook for 4–5 minutes until charred, turning them regularly to ensure an even colouring.

**Remove** to a serving dish, pour over the mimosa dressing and serve warm.

**PER SERVING:** 142 KCALS, 11G FAT, 2G SATURATED FAT, 0.08G SODIUM

# stuffed aubergine with tomato and bulghur pilaff

This always makes an impressive-looking dish, stuffed with all manner of ingredients. Bulghur or cracked wheat is a staple of the Balkan countries where it is used as a cheaper alternative to rice.

4 medium aubergines
2 garlic cloves, thinly sliced
½ teaspoon olive oil
1 red onion, chopped
1 tablespoon thyme leaves
125g sun-blush tomatoes
50g raisins

125g bulghur (cracked wheat) cooked
2 tablespoons pine kernels, toasted
1 tablespoon roughly chopped coriander leaves
50g half-fat Cheddar cheese, grated
Freshly ground black pepper

**Serves 4**

**Preheat** the oven to 200°C/400°F/gas mark 6.

**With** a sharp knife, make slits all over the aubergine and, using half the garlic, stud a slice of garlic into each slit. Wrap the aubergines in a large sheet of foil and seal the foil. Place on a baking sheet and cook in the oven for 30 minutes. When cooked, remove from the foil, cut in half horizontally and allow to cool completely.

**Remove** the aubergine flesh from the centres, leaving enough outer wall to keep the aubergines intact. Chop the flesh into large dice.

**Heat** the olive oil in a non-stick pan, add the onion, remaining garlic and the thyme. Cook until lightly golden.

**Add** the aubergine flesh, tomatoes, raisins, the cooked bulghur and 100ml water, cover with a lid and cook over a low heat for 10 minutes. Add the pine kernels, the coriander and Cheddar. Season with black pepper to taste.
Fill the aubergine casings with the mix, place on a baking sheet, return to the oven and bake for 15 minutes.

PER SERVING:
301 KCALS, 8G FAT, 2G SATURATED FAT, 0.41G SODIUM

# chickpea dolmades

This recipe uses chickpeas as a substitute for the traditional meaty filling.

20 fresh vine leaves
1 tablespoon olive oil
1 onion, finely chopped
1 garlic clove, crushed
50g mint, chopped
100g feta cheese, crumbled
425g tinned chickpeas, drained and rinsed
50g pine kernels
150g brown rice, cooked
½ teaspoon ground cumin
50g currants
Oil-water spray (see page 33)

**For the tomato tartare**
310g ripe plum tomatoes, deseeded and cut into 1cm dice
1 tablespoon maple syrup
Juice of ½ small lemon
2 tablespoons chopped coriander
2 tablespoons chopped parsley
1 garlic clove, crushed

**For the yogurt sauce**
100ml low-fat natural yogurt
2 tablespoons chopped mint
½ teaspoon grated lemon zest
1 tablespoon honey

**Serves 4**

**Preheat** the oven to 180°C/350°F/gas mark 4. Blanch the fresh vine leaves for 3–4 minutes in boiling water until tender. Drain well and pat dry on kitchen paper.

**Heat** the olive oil in a pan, add the onion, garlic and 2 tablespoons water, cover and cook over a low heat for 3–4 minutes. Uncover, add the mint, half the feta, chickpeas, pine kernels, rice, cumin, currants and cook for 2–3 minutes. Allow to cool slightly.

**Place** the vine leaves, shiny-side down, on a work surface. Spoon some of the rice filling in the centre and fold the stalk end over the filling. Roll up the parcel towards the tip of the leaf, tucking in the sides. Lightly grease a baking tray with the oil-water spray, sprinkle over the remaining feta cheese and place under a preheated grill to melt for 1–2 minutes.

**To** make the tartare, mix together all the ingredients in a bowl. Do the same for the yogurt sauce. Dress the grilled vine leaves with the tomato tartare, drizzle over a little sauce and serve.

PER SERVING:
410 KCALS, 20G FAT, 5G SATURATED FAT, 0.54G SODIUM

# 'wild' baguette with mozzarella cheese fondue

A tastier version of cheese on toast, this makes a great snack at any time of the day. If you find wild mushrooms a little expensive or hard to find, replace with another variety; the dish will be equally delicious.

½ large French baguette
1 teaspoon olive oil
200g selection of wild mushrooms, thickly sliced
2 shallots, finely chopped
½ garlic clove, roasted
50g rocket leaves, chopped
2 tablespoons roughly chopped flat-leaf parsley
Freshly ground black pepper

**For the mozzarella fondue**
150ml semi-skimmed milk
1 garlic clove, crushed
2 tablespoons cornflour
Pinch of paprika
½ teaspoon Dijon mustard
75g half-fat mozzarella cheese, grated

**Serves 4**

**Preheat** the grill to its highest setting. Cut the baguette in half, then in half horizontally to create bread bases.

**Heat** the olive oil in a non-stick frying pan, then add the mushrooms, shallots and garlic and cook for 3–4 minutes until tender and golden. Add the chopped rocket and parsley, season with black pepper and keep warm.

**To** make the fondue, boil the milk with the garlic in a pan. Dilute the cornflour with 2 tablespoons water and whisk into the milk. Cook for 2 minutes, then add the paprika and mustard. Remove from the heat and stir in the grated mozzarella. Stir until the cheese has melted into the sauce.

**Toast** the baguettes under the grill, top with the mushrooms, drizzle over the cheese fondue and serve.

PER SERVING: 235 KCALS, 5G FAT, 2G SATURATED FAT, 0.35G SODIUM

# grilled portobello burger with ricotta and rocket slaw

A great vegetarian burger using juicy Portobello mushrooms that have an almost meaty flavour of their own. Good for summer barbecues where vegetarians needn't feel left out.

4 medium/large Portobello mushrooms, stalks removed
2 garlic cloves, peeled
1 teaspoon thyme leaves
2 tablespoons balsamic vinegar
1 teaspoon olive oil
4 traditional burger buns, split open

**Serves 4**

**For the herbed ricotta**
1 tablespoon pesto
4 tablespoons ricotta cheese

**For the rocket slaw**
75g rocket leaves
1 tablespoon balsamic vinegar
2 tablespoons reduced-calorie mayonnaise
2 spring onions, shredded
1 small carrot, peeled and sliced
1 tablespoon honey

**Clean** and peel the mushrooms. Using a small paring knife, cut slits into the mushrooms.

**Cut** the garlic cloves into thin slices, then push into the holes in the mushrooms. Place in a dish, sprinkle over the thyme, pour over the vinegar and oil and leave to marinate for 1 hour. Meanwhile, to make the herbed ricotta, mix the pesto with the ricotta and set aside. Mix all the ingredients for the rocket slaw together in a bowl.

**Heat** a grill pan or griddle and, when smoking, add the mushrooms and grill for 3–4 minutes on each side until soft, cooked and slightly charred all over. Remove, then toast the buns until charred, this should take 2–3 minutes.

**Spread** the buns with the herbed ricotta and add a grilled Portobello. Top with a spoonful of rocket slaw, then replace the bun lid and serve. Oven fries (see page 101) are a classic accompaniment.

PER SERVING:
236 KCALS, 9G FAT, 3G SATURATED FAT, 0.39G SODIUM

# shiitaki mushroom noodles with asian pesto

Pesto is a classic Italian sauce redolent of garlic, lots of basil and Parmesan. My Asian variety uses mint and coriander spiced with ginger and is great for a salad dressing or served with grilled fish.

400g Chinese egg noodles
1 tablespoon sesame oil
125g shiitake mushrooms, thickly sliced
1 garlic clove, crushed
1cm piece of root ginger, peeled and finely chopped
1 green chilli, deseeded and thinly sliced
4 spring onions, shredded
40ml reduced-salt soy sauce

## For the pesto
40g mint leaves
40g coriander leaves
1 garlic clove, crushed
25g roasted peanuts
2.5cm piece root ginger, peeled and finely chopped
1 tablespoon olive oil
Pinch of sugar

Serves 4

**To** make the pesto, place all the ingredients in a blender, blitz to a coarse purée and set aside.

**Soak** the noodles for 3–4 minutes in a bowl of boiling water, then drain them well.

**In** a large non-stick pan or wok, heat the sesame oil until very hot, then add the sliced shiitake mushrooms and sauté for 1 minute or until they are slightly softened. Add the garlic, ginger and chilli and continue to stir-fry. Add the spring onions and soy sauce and toss together.

**Add** the drained noodles and the pesto, toss together until heated through and serve.

PER SERVING:
499 KCALS, 17G FAT, 3G SATURATED FAT, 0.66G SODIUM

# menemen (turkish scrambled eggs)

This recipe comes courtesy of a friend who took a lot of persuading to divulge it. It's a great way to start the day or an ideal snack for lunchtime served with traditional Turkish bread. Adding a little diced feta is good but will raise the fat count.

1 teaspoon olive oil
1 onion, finely chopped
½ garlic clove, crushed
1 teaspoon harissa (hot spice paste)
1 small aubergine, cut into 1cm cubes
1 small green pepper, deseeded and cut into 1cm cubes
2 plum tomatoes, cut into 1cm cubes
2 large free-range eggs
Freshly ground black pepper
Good pinch of saffron, dissolved in 2 tablespoons boiling water
2 tablespoons chopped coriander leaves

Serves 4

**Heat** the olive oil in a medium-sized non-stick frying pan. Add the onion, garlic and harissa and cook over a low heat for 1–2 minutes until softened, stirring regularly. Add the vegetables and cook for 10–15 minutes.

**Meanwhile** in a bowl whisk the eggs with black pepper and add the saffron water.

**When** the vegetables are cooked, raise the heat, add the eggs and allow them to set slightly before stirring them to make chunky scrambled eggs around the vegetables. Add the coriander and more pepper to taste. Serve with Middle-Eastern-style bread.

PER SERVING:
89 KCALS, 5G FAT, 1G SATURATED FAT, 0.06G SODIUM

# indo-chine stir-fried rice with paneer and cashews

Everyone loves rice and has their preferred cooking method, but I especially love the oriental way of stir-frying it. Paneer is a curd cheese, which is widely available in supermarkets.

1 tablespoon unsaturated oil
3 cardamom pods, cracked
½ teaspoon ground cinnamon
2 spring onions, chopped
1 red chilli, deseeded and finely chopped
50g ready-to-eat dried apricots, chopped
40g sultanas
1 teaspoon curry powder
300g basmati rice, cooked
50g paneer (curd cheese), cut into 1cm dice
50g fresh cashew nuts, chopped and toasted
25g mint, chopped

**Serves 4**

Heat a large non-stick frying pan or wok and add the oil, spices, spring onions and chilli and cook for 1 minute. Add the apricots, sultanas and curry powder and cook for 1 minute.

Add the cooked rice, paneer and cashews and toss together for 2–3 minutes. Remove to a serving bowl and sprinkle with the mint before serving.

**PER SERVING:**
273 KCALS, 11G FAT, 2G SATURATED FAT, 0.07G SODIUM

# pad tofu

This vegetarian stir-fried rice noodle dish is one of countless Thai variations on a theme, both interesting and tasty, and the tofu provides valuable soya protein. Pickled white radish is available in tins and can be sourced from Asian grocers.

310g vermicelli rice noodles
1 tablespoon peanut (groundnut) oil
2 garlic cloves, crushed
½ tablespoon finely chopped root ginger
1 red chilli, thinly sliced
310g Chinese broccoli, trimmed and chopped into pieces
100g bean sprouts
2 tablespoons chopped pickled white radish
1 tablespoon brown sugar
20ml reduced-salt soy sauce
1 tablespoon sweet chilli sauce
4 spring onions, shredded
175g firm tofu
2 tablespoons roughly chopped coriander leaves
2 tablespoons chopped roasted peanuts
Freshly ground black pepper

**Serves 4**

Place the rice noodles in a bowl, cover with boiling water, leave to soften and then drain them well.

In a wok or large non-stick frying pan, heat the peanut oil, add the garlic, ginger and chilli and stir-fry for 1 minute.

Add the broccoli, bean sprouts and radish and cook for a further minute. Add the sugar, soy and chilli sauces and toss well together.

Throw in the spring onions, tofu, coriander and peanuts. Season with black pepper to taste and serve in bowls.

**PER SERVING:**
401 KCALS, 8G FAT, 1G SATURATED FAT, 0.34G SODIUM

# wasabi tuna tartare with cucumber and orange, and beetroot syrup

I love the freshness and contrasts of flavour in this dish, the sweet beetroot syrup, then the hot wasabi horseradish, adding punch to the raw tuna tartare.

**For the tartare**
175g very fresh tuna fillet,
  cut into 5mm dice
1 shallot, finely chopped
Zest and juice of 1 orange
75g cucumber, peeled and
  deseeded, cut into
  5mm dice
2 tablespoons chopped coriander
  leaves, plus extra to garnish

½ teaspoon wasabi paste
1 tablespoon chopped chives
2 tablespoons reduced-salt
  soy sauce
Freshly ground black pepper

**For the beetroot syrup**
2 raw beetroots
5 tablespoons sherry vinegar
  or red wine vinegar
½ teaspoon Dijon mustard

**Serves 4**

**To** make the beetroot syrup, peel the beetroots (I suggest you wear a pair of kitchen gloves if you have them!), place in a juicer and extract the juice.

**Place** the juice in a pan with the vinegar and bring to the boil, skimming off any impurities that rise to the surface. Boil until the liquid has reduced by half.

**Pour** into a bowl and allow to cool. Whisk in the mustard and season with black pepper to taste, then set aside.

**To** make the tartare, place the tuna in a bowl, add the remaining ingredients and season with black pepper to taste. Place a 6cm cookie cutter on a serving plate, fill with the mix, press down well, then carefully remove the ring. Prepare the remaining three in the same way.

**Pour** some beetroot syrup around each tartare, garnish with the coriander leaves and serve chilled.

**PER SERVING:**
85 KCALS, 2G FAT, 1G SATURATED FAT, 0.39G SODIUM

# dhal cakes on asian-style panzanella

Don't be put off by the large list of ingredients in this recipe; it is simple to prepare and a vegetarian delight. The cakes may be prepared in advance and cooked when needed. A wonderful dish for the summer months.

150g split yellow lentils, soaked overnight
1 teaspoon olive oil
1 garlic clove, crushed
1 green chilli, deseeded and finely chopped
½ teaspoon ground cumin
2½cm piece of root ginger, finely chopped
125g couscous
75g spinach, chopped and cooked
75g low-fat cottage cheese
2 spring onions, chopped
2 tablespoons chopped mint
Oil-water spray (see page 33)

### For the asian panzanella
1 tablespoon honey
1 mango, peeled and cut into 1cm dice
1 naan bread, cut into 1cm pieces
Juice of 2 limes
1 red pepper, deseeded and cut into 1cm dice
½ garlic clove, crushed
1 green chilli, deseeded and finely chopped
2 tablespoons chopped coriander leaves

### For the mint dressing
1 tablespoon mint jelly, melted
100ml soya yogurt

Serves 4

**Drain** the soaked lentils. Heat the oil in a non-stick pan, add the garlic, chilli and cumin and cook for 1 minute to release their fragrance. Add the lentils, ginger and 65ml water, then cover and cook for 10–15 minutes or until the lentils are tender and all the liquid has been absorbed.

**Meanwhile**, boil 370ml water and pour over the couscous, cover with clingfilm and leave to stand for 4–5 minutes. Fluff the couscous with a fork and leave to swell for a further 5 minutes, until all the liquid is completely absorbed. Remove the clingfilm and allow to cool completely.

**Place** the lentils and the couscous in a blender, add the chopped spinach, mix well, then in short bursts, pulse to a coarse pulp. Do not purée completely. Remove the mix to a bowl, add the cottage cheese, spring onions and mint, mix well and place in the fridge.

**Preheat** the grill to the highest setting.

**Divide** the mix into patties. Lightly spray a baking tray with the oil-water spray, then arrange the patties on the tray. Grill the patties for 2–3 minutes on each side.

**Meanwhile**, to make the panzanella, mix all the ingredients together in a bowl.

**To** make the dressing, mix together the mint jelly and yogurt. To serve, arrange the panzanella on a large serving dish, top with the grilled dhal cakes, and drizzle with the mint dressing.

PER SERVING:
461 KCALS, 9G FAT, 3G SATURATED FAT, 0.25G SODIUM

# steamed mussels with fragrant asian spices

Mussels are a delicate mollusc; they need a minimum of cooking to retain their juicy and moist flavours. The addition of some basic Indian spices leaves the kitchen filled with heady aromas.

1 teaspoon cumin seeds
2 teaspoons cardamom pods, cracked
1kg very fresh mussels, cleaned and beards removed
2 shallots, finely chopped
90ml dry white wine
2½cm piece of root ginger, peeled and finely chopped
1 green chilli, deseeded and finely chopped
2 tablespoons roughly chopped coriander leaves

**Serves 4**

**Heat** a large non-stick wok (with a tight-fitting lid). Add the cumin seeds and cardamom pods, and cook for 30 seconds to release their fragrance.

**Throw** in the mussels, add the shallots, white wine, ginger and chilli and 150ml water. Cover with the lid, bring to the boil rapidly and steam the mussels for 2–3 minutes until they open.

**Add** the coriander and toss well together. Discard any unopened mussels and serve in a deep bowl with the broth poured over.

PER SERVING:
84 KCALS, 2G FAT, 0G SATURATED FAT, 0.22G SODIUM

# mackerel tartare in tomato shells

This is a light meal in itself, but can be a great starter for a dinner party as it can be prepared up to 2 hours ahead of time, leaving you plenty of time for your guests. Tuna or salmon could easily be used instead.

8 medium/large salad tomatoes
Freshly ground black pepper
4 tablespoons olive oil
2 x 350g very fresh mackerel, cleaned and filleted
1 teaspoon Dijon mustard
Juice of 2 lemons
1 small head fennel, very finely chopped
2 shallots, finely chopped
2 tablespoons chopped mint
2 tablespoons chopped tarragon leaves
2 tablespoons chopped chives
1 small cooked beetroot, peeled and very finely chopped

**Serves 4**

**Preheat** the oven to 180°C/350°F/gas mark 4.

**Carefully** slice the tops off of the tomatoes and scoop out the flesh and seeds and discard. Dry the insides of the tomatoes gently with kitchen paper, and season with black pepper. Brush inside and out with 1 tablespoon of the olive oil and cook in the oven for 5–8 minutes until they are just softened, but still retaining their shape. Remove and allow to cool.

**Cut** the mackerel fillet into 1cm dice and place in a bowl. Add the mustard, lemon juice, fennel, remaining olive oil, the shallots and herbs and gently toss together. Add the beetroot and season with pepper to taste.

**Fill** the tomato shells with the mackerel tartare. Serve with a fresh green salad.

PER SERVING:
462 KCALS, 35G FAT, 6G SATURATED FAT, 0.16G SODIUM

# ceviche of salmon and shellfish

Ceviche is a Central and South American speciality, in which raw fish is marinated in lime or lemon juice, and is a healthy way to start a dinner party.

2 beefsteak tomatoes
2 fresh red chillies, deseeded and chopped
Juice of 2 limes
1 teaspoon coriander seeds, crushed
100ml tomato juice
½ teaspoon sugar
Tabasco sauce
Freshly ground black pepper

300g fresh wild salmon fillet, skinned
250g cooked seafood selection
50g cucumber, peeled, deseeded and diced
4 spring onions, chopped
1 tablespoon chopped coriander
Sprigs of coriander and lime wedges, to garnish

**Serves 4**

**Preheat** the grill to its highest setting. Cut one of the tomatoes in half, place the cut side down on a baking tray and grill until the skins blacken. Turn over and blacken the other side. Remove and allow to cool.

**Soak** the remaining tomato in boiling water for about 1 minute, then remove with a slotted spoon. Peel away the skin, deseed and dice. Set aside.

**Blend** the charred tomato with the chillies, lime juice, coriander seeds, tomato juice, sugar and a dash of Tabasco until puréed and smooth, then season with pepper. Strain through a sieve.

**Cut** the salmon into thin slices and season lightly with pepper. Place in the bowl with the marinade and the shellfish, cover with clingfilm and marinate in the refrigerator for 2 hours.

**Remove** the salmon and shellfish from the marinade and arrange on 4 plates. Add the cucumber, spring onions, chopped coriander and reserved diced tomato to the marinade and pour a little over the fish. Garnish each plate with a coriander leaf and a wedge of lime and serve chilled.

PER SERVING:
229 KCALS, 9G FAT, 2G SATURATED FAT, 0.75G SODIUM

# thin sardine tart

A delicate and light tart base, topped with sardines – a play on the classic pissaladière from southern France. Filo is less fattening than puff pastry, and it is wonderfully crispy. Altogether a great starter or lunchtime dish.

Oil-water spray (see page 33)
4 filo pastry sheets
1 tablespoon olive oil
1 large onion, thinly sliced
2 garlic cloves, crushed

1 tablespoon black olives, pitted and roughly chopped
2 tinned anchovy fillets, drained, rinsed and finely chopped
8 fresh sardines, cleaned, scaled and filleted
1 teaspoon thyme leaves
2 tablespoons chopped parsley

**Serves 4**

**Preheat** the oven to 200°C/400°F/gas mark 6. Warm a 23cm baking tin or pizza tin in the oven. Remove and spray with the oil-water spray.

**Place** one sheet of filo in the tin then lightly spray all over, top with a second sheet, spray again, top with a third sheet, spray again, then top with the last sheet. Place in the oven for 2–3 minutes, then remove. Crumple up the excess pastry overhanging the tin to form a rim.

**Heat** the olive oil in a large non-stick pan, add the onion, garlic and olives and cook over a moderate heat for 10–12 minutes until the onions are soft, golden and caramelised. Remove from the pan, add the anchovies and mix well.

**Wipe** out the pan. Return to the heat and squirt with a little oil-water spray. Fry the sardine fillets for 2–3 minutes until golden and lightly crisp.

**Spread** the onion mix evenly over the filo base, then arrange the cooked sardine fillets on top. Scatter over the thyme and return to the oven for 2–3 minutes. Sprinkle over the parsley and serve on a large dish with a bowl of green salad.

PER SERVING:
310 KCALS, 14G FAT, 3G SATURATED FAT, 0.44G SODIUM

# 4

# main courses

# spicy aubergine and shiitake stew

A simply prepared dish, packed with flavour. Stews are a good way to cook vegetables as their nutrients are retained in the liquid. The shiitake mushroom may be replaced with any mushroom variety, but shiitakes will instill a meaty flavour to this dish.

1 tablespoon sesame oil
2 garlic cloves, crushed
2½cm piece of root ginger, peeled and finely chopped
200g shiitake mushrooms, thickly sliced
3 tablespoons dry sherry
2 tablespoons ketchap manis (Indonesian soy sauce)
2 tablespoons black bean sauce
2 large aubergines, cut into 2½cm dice
1 tin water chestnuts, sliced
600ml vegetable stock (see page 39)
100ml tomato juice

**Serves 4**

**Heat** a wok or large frying pan, add the sesame oil, garlic, ginger and mushrooms and cook over a high heat for 1–2 minutes.

**Add** the sherry, ketchap manis and black bean sauce and mix well together. Add the aubergines, water chestnuts and mix well again. Cook for 3-4 minutes, then add the stock and tomato juice. Cover with a lid, reduce the heat and simmer for 5–8 minutes until the vegetables are cooked, but still retain their shape and the sauce is reduced in consistency.

**Serve** with a bowl of steaming white rice.

**PER SERVING:**
97 KCALS, 4G FAT, 0G SATURATED FAT, 0.83G SODIUM

# indian vegetable crumble

1 small cauliflower, separated into florets
1 onion, chopped
2 garlic cloves, crushed
5cm piece of root ginger
1 hot green chilli, deseeded and finely chopped
Oil-water spray (see page 33)
2 tablespoons tandoori spice mix
100g paneer (curd cheese), drained and diced
2 carrots, cut into batons
1 red pepper, deseeded, diced
1 green pepper, deseeded, diced
1 baking potato, peeled, diced

425g tinned chickpeas, drained and rinsed
2 tablespoons roughly chopped coriander

**For the crumble crust**
100g fresh cashew nuts
½ teaspoon mild curry powder
50g cooked millet seed
1 teaspoon olive oil

**For the mint yogurt sauce**
100ml low-fat natural yogurt
2 tablespoons roughly chopped mint
1 tablespoon lemon juice
Pinch of ground cumin

**Serves 4**

**Preheat** the oven to 190°C/375°F/gas mark 5. Cook the cauliflower florets for 5 minutes in a pan of boiling water. Remove and refresh in cold water, drain and dry well. Place the onion, garlic, ginger and green chilli in a blender with 65ml water and blitz to a purée.

**In** a non-stick pan, heat a squirt of oil-water spray, then add the tandoori spice and paneer and cook for 1 minute.

**Add** the cauliflower and remaining vegetables, the chickpeas and mix well together. Add 65ml water, cover and simmer for 6–8 minutes. Add the garlic and chilli mixture and cook uncovered until the vegetables are all coated in spices, this should take about 5 minutes. Transfer the vegetables to a small gratin or baking dish, suitable for oven-to-table use.

**To** make the crumble crust, coarsely blitz the cashews with the curry powder, millet and olive oil in a blender.

**Sprinkle** the mix evenly over the vegetables, then bake in the oven for 12–15 minutes until the crust is golden and crispy. Mix the sauce ingredients together. Remove the crumble from the oven, scatter with the chopped coriander and serve with the yogurt mint sauce.

**PER SERVING:**
463 KCALS, 21G FAT, 4G SATURATED FAT, 0.34G SODIUM

# baked corn and vegetable tacos

These rolled tacos filled with vegetables are ideal for preparing ahead. Flour tortillas can be used instead of making corn pancakes to save time.

425g mixed vegetables
  (e.g. parsnips, carrots, butternut
  squash, courgettes)
2 tablespoons honey
1 tablespoon olive oil
1 red chilli, deseeded and
  finely chopped
Freshly ground black pepper

**Serves 4**

Oil-water spray (see page 33)
450ml passata sauce
50g half-fat Cheddar
  cheese, grated

**For the pancakes**
1 large free-range egg
115ml soya milk
1 tablespoon olive oil
30g finely ground cornmeal
45g plain flour

**Preheat** the oven to 200°C/400°F/gas mark 6. Peel the vegetables and cut into large wedges. Tip into a baking tin. Warm the honey, olive oil and chilli together and pour over the vegetables. Toss well, then season with pepper. Place in the oven and roast for 40–45 minutes until golden and slightly caramelised.

**For** the pancakes, lightly beat the egg with the milk, olive oil and 65ml water. Sift in the cornmeal and flour, then gradually mix with the liquid to form a smooth batter. Strain and set aside.

**Heat** a small non-stick pancake or omelette pan. Squirt with a little oil-water spray, then pour 2 tablespoons of batter into the centre of the pan, tilting it quickly so that it spreads into a circle. Cook for 1 minute on each side, loosening the edges of the pancake with a palette knife. Slip on to a plate. Prepare 7 more pancakes in the same way.

**Divide** the roasted vegetables between the 8 pancakes and roll them up tightly. Arrange the pancakes, seam-side down, in a baking dish. Pour over the passata sauce, then sprinkle over the cheese. Bake in the oven until heated through, and the cheese has melted and is bubbling. Serve immediately.

PER SERVING:
281 KCALS, 12G FAT, 3G SATURATED FAT, 0.35G SODIUM

# three-squash ratatouille

I have always been a lover of squash and there are so many varieties available throughout the year. Butternut and turban squash are both winter varieties, which are good sources of iron and vitamins A and C. This makes a great vegetarian meal, served with rice.

2 teaspoons olive oil
3 spring onions, chopped
3 garlic cloves
1 green pepper, deseeded and cut into 2.5cm dice
250g butternut squash, deseeded and cut into 2.5cm dice
250g turban squash, deseeded and cut into 2.5cm dice
2 courgettes, thickly sliced
400g tinned tomatoes, chopped
1 tablespoon tomato purée
1 tablespoon sugar
1 bay leaf
1 tablespoon chopped basil
1 teaspoon thyme leaves
Zest of ½ lemon
Freshly ground black pepper

**Serves 4**

**Preheat** the oven to 160°C/325°F/gas mark 3.

**Heat** the olive oil in an ovenproof non-stick pan, add the spring onions, garlic and green pepper and cook over a moderate heat for 3–4 minutes or until tender.

**Add** all the squash and courgettes, cover with a lid and cook for a further 5 minutes. Add the tomatoes and their juice and the rest of the ingredients. Cover again and cook in the oven for 30 minutes, or until all the vegetables are tender. Remove the bay leaf before serving.

PER SERVING:
111 KCALS, 2G FAT, 0G SATURATED FAT, 0.1G SODIUM

# creamy hazelnut fettuccine with celery and soft herbs

Pasta and nuts have a great affinity, especially when used with fresh herbs too. Other noodle-type pastas such as tagliatelle or pappardelle may be substituted for the fettuccine.

50g whole blanched hazelnuts, lightly toasted
150ml ricotta cheese
2 garlic cloves, crushed
1 teaspoon olive oil
1 shallot, finely chopped
2 sticks celery, peeled and finely diced
450g fresh or dried fettuccini
Freshly ground black pepper
Ground nutmeg
1 tablespoon roughly chopped flat-leaf parsley
1 tablespoon roughly chopped basil

**Serves 4**

**Place** the hazelnuts, cheese and garlic in a blender and blitz to a smooth paste.

**Heat** the olive oil in a pan, add the shallot and celery and 2 tablespoons water, cover with a lid and cook over a low heat until the water is absorbed and vegetables have softened.

**Cook** the pasta in boiling water until al dente and season with pepper and nutmeg. Add the hazelnut sauce and toss well together, then add the parsley and basil, toss again and serve.

PER SERVING:
540 KCALS, 15G FAT, 4G SATURATED FAT, 0.06G SODIUM

# saffron-roasted garlic gnocchi with fennel caponata

These gnocchi are a little time consuming, but worth it. Fresh saffron may be replaced with a little powdered saffron; the flavour is not as good, but it is cheaper and does the job.

900g Maris Piper potatoes, peeled and cut into chunks
Good pinch of saffron, dissolved in 1 tablespoon boiling water
1 teaspoon roasted garlic purée (see page 38)
Freshly ground black pepper
275g plain flour
1 free-range egg
Handful basil leaves

**For the caponata**
1 tablespoon olive oil
2 fennel, heads cut into 1cm dice
12 black olives, pitted and halved
2 tablespoons balsamic vinegar
75g sun-blush tomatoes
½ teaspoon caster sugar

**Serves 4**

**Place** the potatoes in a pan, cover with water and bring to the boil. Cook until tender, drain well, then return to the pan and dry over a low heat. Rub the potatoes through a fine sieve. Add the saffron, water and garlic purée. Season with black pepper and mix well.

**Add** the flour and egg, then mix to a smooth dough. Using floured hands, roll the dough into a 2cm cylinder, then cut into 2cm lengths. With a fork, make an indentation on each piece. Place the gnocchi on a floured tray until ready to cook.

**To** make the caponata, heat the oil in a pan, add the fennel with 2 tablespoons water, cover and cook until the fennel is tender and the water has evaporated. Add the olives, vinegar, tomatoes and sugar, cook for a further 10 minutes, season with black pepper to taste and keep warm.

**Cook** the gnocchi in a pan of boiling water until they rise to the surface, then remove with a slotted spoon and drain well. Dress the gnocchi with the fennel caponata, sprinkle over the torn basil leaves and serve.

PER SERVING:
498 KCALS, 7G FAT, 1G SATURATED FAT, 0.47G SODIUM

# summer vegetable tagliatelle with lemon and tarragon

It is as easy to buy fresh pasta as dried, although nowadays the quality of dried pasta is excellent. This dish is also great served cold, tossed with a spoonful or two of vinaigrette.

Juice of ½ lemon
1 tablespoon olive oil
1 teaspoon honey
2 spring onions, finely chopped
2 tablespoons roughly chopped tarragon

200g asparagus
100g baby courgettes, cut into thick slices
50g fresh or frozen peas
500g fresh or 450g dried tagliatelle
12 sun-blush tomatoes
Freshly ground black pepper

**Serves 4**

**Prepare** a light lemon dressing by whisking together in a bowl the lemon juice, olive oil, honey, spring onions and tarragon. Break off the woody end stems of the asparagus and, using a potato peeler, carefully peel the tips. Cut into 2.5cm lengths.

**Cook** the asparagus for 2 minutes in boiling water, then remove with a slotted spoon and quickly refresh in cold water. Cook the courgettes in the boiling water for 1 minute, remove and quickly refresh in cold water. Add the peas to the boiling water and cook for 2–3 minutes, remove and quickly refresh.

**Cook** the fresh pasta in plenty of boiling water for 2–3 minutes until al dente (dried pasta will need a little longer). Drain the pasta, reserving 65ml of the cooking water, then return the pasta to the pan, add the drained asparagus, courgette and peas with the tomatoes and toss well.

**Add** the lemon dressing and reserved pasta water, season with black pepper to taste, toss well together and serve.

PER SERVING:
420 KCALS, 7G FAT, 1G SATURATED FAT, 0.16G SODIUM

# casarecce pasta with grilled red peppers and peas

Casarecce is a hand-rolled pasta that has been formed in a twist. It is available from Italian delicatessens. Other tubular or twisted varieties can also be used, of course.

2 tablespoons olive oil
2 large red peppers
100g fresh or frozen peas
450g dried casarecce pasta
5 tablespoons half-fat crème fraîche
2 tablespoons chopped basil
Freshly ground black pepper

**Serves 4**

**Preheat** the grill pan until hot, then brush the surface with 1 tablespoon of the oil. Grill the red peppers for 8–10 minutes until charred all over. Remove the peppers and place in a plastic bag for 2–3 minutes until the skins loosen, then remove from the bag, peel and cut into wide strips.

**Cook** the peas in boiling water for 2 minutes until tender, refresh in cold water, drain and dry well.

**Cook** the pasta in plenty of boiling water for 10–12 minutes until al dente. Drain well.

**While** the pasta is cooking, heat the remaining oil in a non-stick frying pan, add the pepper strips and crème fraîche and cook for 1 minute. Add the peas, basil and pasta, and toss the lot together. Season with black pepper to taste and serve immediately.

PER SERVING:
518 KCALS, 11G FAT, 3G SATURATED FAT, 0.04G SODIUM

# aubergine, green olive and preserved lemon risotto

This is a vegetarian risotto with a Moroccan feel. Although there are many types of risotto rice, I prefer Vialamo Namo. It has a great flavour, and low starch content, which keeps the grains firm and moist.

1 tablespoon olive oil
1 aubergine, cut into 2.5cm cubes and blanched
1 onion, finely chopped
200g Vialamo Namo risotto rice
700ml hot vegetable stock (see page 39)
12 plump green olives, pitted
1 tablespoon finely chopped preserved lemon
2 tablespoons roughly chopped flat-leaf parsley
Freshly ground black pepper

**Serves 4**

**Heat** the oil in a large non-stick pan. When hot, add the aubergine and onion and fry for 4–5 minutes until they are lightly browned.

**Add** the rice and stir to mix with the vegetables. Add the vegetable stock, a ladleful at a time, stirring constantly until each amount is absorbed before adding more, until all the stock is used up. Cook for 20–25 minutes.

**Add** the olives, lemon and parsley, season with pepper to taste and serve.

**Should** you have any risotto left over, it makes a great salad tossed with a little low-fat vinaigrette.

**PER SERVING:**
237 KCALS, 6G FAT, 1G SATURATED FAT, 0.5G SODIUM

# oven-baked pumpkin risotto

A recipe for a risotto that does away with the boredom of the continual stirring usually needed for risottos. Once it is in the oven, simply leave it to cook while you attend to other things. Pumpkin is very popular at the moment and contains lots of beta-carotene.

450g pumpkin, peeled and cut into 1cm dice
1 small onion, finely chopped
1 garlic clove, crushed
Oil-water spray (see page 33)
Freshly ground black pepper
200g Vialamo Namo risotto rice
Zest of ½ lemon
700ml hot vegetable stock (see page 39)
30g Parmesan cheese, finely grated

**Serves 4**

**Preheat** the oven to 200°C/400°F/gas mark 6.

**Place** the pumpkin, onion and garlic in a non-stick ovenproof casserole dish. Spray the vegetables lightly with the oil-water spray and season lightly with black pepper. Place in the oven for 15–20 minutes, until golden and caramelised, turning regularly.

**Sprinkle** over the rice and lemon zest and stir it all together. Pour over the boiling stock and stir well. Cover with foil and return to the oven for 25–30 minutes or until the rice is tender and all the stock is absorbed.

**Stir** in half of the Parmesan, scatter the remainder over the top and serve immediately.

**PER SERVING:**
228 KCALS, 3G FAT, 2G SATURATED FAT, 0.31G SODIUM

# almond-crumbed fish with baked oven fries and cumin ketchup

We all love fish and chips, but they contain a lot of fat traditionally, so here is my low-fat recipe. Panko crumbs are coarse Japanese breadcrumbs and can be sourced from Oriental stores.

**For the fish**
75g panko crumbs or
  breadcrumbs
50g nibbed almonds
½ teaspoon ground cumin
½ teaspoon ground coriander
¼ teaspoon smoked paprika
Pinch of ground turmeric
Freshly ground black pepper
4 x 175g cleaned halibut
  fillets, each cut into
  2 finger-sized pieces

40g plain flour
2 egg whites, lightly beaten
Oil-water spray (see page 33)
1 lemon, sliced, to garnish

**For the fries**
600g baking potatoes
1 teaspoon unsaturated oil
1 large egg white, lightly beaten

**For the cumin ketchup**
2 tablespoons low-fat natural yogurt
½ teaspoon ground cumin
90ml tomato ketchup

Serves 4

**Preheat** the oven to 200°C/400°F/gas mark 6. To make the fries, cut the washed potatoes into equal-sized wedges, dry them well, then dip in the egg white until they are thoroughly coated. Place in a non-stick baking tin, skin-side down, and bake for 40–45 minutes until cooked and golden brown.

**Combine** the panko crumbs, almonds and spices together in a bowl with a little pepper. Season the fish, then dredge with flour before passing them through the beaten egg whites, then the spiced crumb mix. Lightly spray the fish with a little oil-water spray, then place in a large non-stick baking tin.

**Place** in the oven to cook until golden, this should take about 5-6 minutes, depending on the thickness of your fish.
To make the cumin ketchup, mix all the ingredients in a bowl and season with black pepper to taste. Serve the fish and chips with the ketchup and some lemon slices to garnish.

PER SERVING:
530 KCALS, 13G FAT, 1G SATURATED FAT, 0.69G SODIUM

# grilled halibut with artichokes, potatoes and chilli parsley sauce

Grilling fish is the perfect way to keep fat to a minimum. Halibut is a fine fish for grilling, tender and juicy and great for summer barbecues.

300g large new potatoes
Oil-water spray (see page 33)
400g tinned artichokes in
  water, drained and halved
1 tablespoon superfine capers,
  drained and rinsed
4 x 175g thick halibut
  fillets, skinned

Serves 4

**For the sauce**
½ teaspoon Dijon mustard
½ small green chilli, deseeded
  and finely chopped
Juice of ½ lemon
1 teaspoon balsamic vinegar
1 teaspoon olive oil
2 tinned anchovy fillets, rinsed and
  finely chopped
2 tablespoons chopped parsley
Freshly ground black pepper

**Place** the potatoes in a pan of boiling water and cook for 15–20 minutes or until just tender. Refresh under cold water, and drain well. Cut the potatoes in half lengthways and set aside.

**To** make the sauce, place the mustard and green chilli, lemon juice and balsamic vinegar in a bowl and mix together. Gradually add the oil, anchovies, 100ml water and the chopped parsley. Mix well together and season to taste with black pepper.

**Heat** a ridged grill pan over a high heat, squirt with a little oil-water spray, then add the potatoes. Cook for 5–6 minutes, turning then regularly during cooking, until golden and slightly charred all over. Remove and keep warm. Do the same with the artichokes, then toss together with the potatoes and capers. Keep warm.

**Season** the halibut fillets, squirt with a little oil-water spray and grill for 2–3 minutes on each side.

**Place** the vegetables on 4 serving plates, top with a grilled halibut fillet, pour over a little sauce and serve.

PER SERVING:
263 KCALS, 5G FAT, 1G SATURATED FAT, 0.39G SODIUM

# baked mustard cod with lemon peel and capers

A variation on a dish first prepared during my early days in the business, while working at the Royal Garden in London. I have never forgotten it, so I include it here for posterity.

Oil-water spray (see page 33)
1 teaspoon Dijon mustard
4 x 175g (6oz) thick cod
   fillets, skinned
4 tomatoes
2 courgettes

**Serves 4**

Juice and zest of ½ lemon
1 tablespoon superfine capers,
   drained and rinsed
65ml dry white wine
150ml fish stock (see page 39)
½ teaspoon picked thyme leaves
1 tablespoon roughly chopped
   tarragon

**Preheat** the oven to 200°C/400°F/gas mark 6.

**Lightly** grease a large non-stick baking tray with the oil-water spray. Brush the mustard lightly over the surface of each fish fillet and place on the tray.

**Slice** the tomatoes and courgettes into 1cm thick slices. Blanch the courgettes in boiling water for 1 minute, drain, refresh in a bowl of cold water and dry them. Lay overlapping slices of tomato and courgette on each fish fillet, alternating them for colour. Sprinkle a little lemon zest and a few capers over each fillet.

**Pour** over the white wine, fish stock and lemon juice and sprinkle the thyme and tarragon over the fish.

**Loosely** cover the tray with foil to secure the juices, and bake in the oven until cooked through, this will take about 5–8 minutes depending on the thickness of the cod.

**When** the fish is cooked remove carefully to serving dishes. Strain any cooking juices and pour any remaining juices over the fish before serving.

PER SERVING:
187 KCALS, 2G FAT, 0G SATURATED FAT, 0.31G SODIUM

# pan-caramelised cod with sweet-and-sour shallots

Cod is a very delicate fish and can be prepared in all manner of ways from baking or poaching to frying and braising, as in my recipe here with sweet-and-sour shallots and ginger.

12 Thai shallots, peeled
65ml reduced-salt light soy sauce
30g brown sugar
65ml white wine vinegar
1 x 5cm piece of root ginger,
   peeled and very finely chopped

**Serves 4**

1 teaspoon coriander seeds
¼ teaspoon freshly ground
   black pepper
4 x 175g cod fillets, skinned
75ml dry white wine
225ml fish stock
   (see page 39)
75ml orange juice
1 tablespoon chopped chives

**Preheat** the oven to 200°C/400°F/gas mark 6. Peel the shallots and cook in a pan of boiling water for 3–4 minutes. Remove with a slotted spoon and refresh in cold water, then dry them well.

**In** a large non-stick ovenproof pan, heat a little of the soy sauce with the sugar and vinegar and bring to the boil. Add the root ginger, coriander seeds and black pepper and cook until the liquid caramelises lightly into a syrup.

**Season** the cod fillets with a little pepper, then add to the syrup. Cook for 2 minutes until the fish begins to caramelise, then turn the fillets over with a palette knife or fish slice.

**Pour** over the white wine, fish stock and orange juice, then tuck in the shallots around the fish. Cover with a lid and place in the oven for 4–5 minutes or until the fish is cooked.

**Remove** the fish carefully from the pan on to serving plates, top with the shallots and pour the sauce over the fish. If the sauce is too thin, reduce it down to a syrup-like consistency that coats the back of a spoon. Sprinkle over the chives and serve with a sweet potato mash made with finely chopped red chillies and, of course, skimmed milk.

PER SERVING:
210 KCALS, 2G FAT, 0G SATURATED FAT, 0.89G SODIUM

# steamed sea bass with ginger and sweet chilli

Sea bass is the king of fish and is usually expensive, but superb for that special dinner party treat. Trout or salmon could easily be used instead, however, with equal success.

Handful of seaweed
2.5cm piece of root ginger, peeled and finely chopped, trimmings retained
2 star anis
4 x 175g thick sea bass fillets, skinned
½ lemongrass stick, very finely chopped

**Serves 4**

**For the broth**
4 spring onions, cut in 2.5cm lengths
8 shiitake mushrooms, sliced
150ml chicken stock (see page 39)
1 garlic clove, crushed
2 tablespoons dry sherry
1 tablespoon reduced-salt soy sauce
2 tablespoons sweet chilli sauce
1 teaspoon sesame oil
2 tablespoons roughly shredded holy basil

**Place** the seaweed, ginger trimmings and star anis in a pan large enough to hold a bamboo steamer on top. Cover with 300ml water, bring to the boil and simmer for 2–3 minutes.

**Place** the sea bass fillets in the base of the steamer and scatter over the finely chopped ginger and lemongrass. Cover with a lid, place over the pan and steam for 5 minutes.

**Meanwhile**, prepare the broth. Put all the ingredients in a pan and bring to the boil, then simmer for 2–3 minutes to meld the flavours.

**Place** the fish in deep serving bowls, pour over the broth and serve with steamed rice and oriental greens such as pak choi or Chinese broccoli.

PER SERVING:
212 KCALS, 5G FAT, 1G SATURATED FAT, 0.57G SODIUM

# cod with sweet pepper and portobello bolognese

For me, cod is one of the greatest and most versatile of fish: it poaches, bakes and deep-fries well and can take lots of diverse flavours to accompany it. This spicy pepper and mushroom sauce is a great example.

Oil-water spray (see page 33)
1 onion, finely diced
1 garlic clove, crushed
1 carrot, finely diced
50g chorizo sausage, finely diced
1 red pepper, roasted, skinned, deseeded and finely chopped
2 Portobello mushrooms, peeled and finely chopped

1 tablespoon thyme leaves
200g tinned tomatoes, chopped
1 teaspoon tomato purée
1 tablespoon brown sugar
65ml red wine
1 teaspoon Worcestershire sauce
4 x 175g cod fillets, skinned
Freshly ground black pepper
Pinch of paprika

**Serves 4**

**To** make the bolognese sauce, add a squirt of oil-water spray to a non-stick frying pan and heat. Add the onion, garlic and carrot and 2 teaspoons water and cover with a lid.

**Cook** for about 5 minutes until the vegetables begin to soften, stirring regularly.

**Add** the chorizo, red pepper, Portobello mushrooms and thyme and cook for a further 5 minutes. Add the tomatoes, tomato purée, brown sugar, red wine and Worcestershire sauce and simmer for 20 minutes over a moderate heat.

**Heat** another non-stick frying pan with a squirt of oil-water spray. Season the cod fillets with black pepper and a pinch of paprika and cook for 3–4 minutes on each side, until golden and crispy. Remove from the pan and serve with the bolognese sauce on a bed of fresh noodles.

PER SERVING:
251 KCALS, 5G FAT, 1G SATURATED FAT, 0.25G SODIUM

# hake with shellfish in green butter

Don't panic! The green butter isn't butter at all; it's the name given to the rich garlicky herb paste, which is so moreish and buttery in taste, but without the fat of course. Cod may be substituted for hake if it is more readily available.

Oil-water spray (see page 33)
4 x 175g hake steaks
Freshly ground black pepper
250g mussels, cleaned and beards removed
250g baby clams, washed
650ml hot fish stock (see page 39)

**For the green butter**
3 garlic cloves, crushed
1 tinned anchovy fillet, drained and rinsed
Handful of flat-leaf parsley

**Serves 4**

**To** make the green butter, blitz the garlic, anchovy and parsley to a smooth paste in a blender. Place in a bowl, cover and keep in the fridge.

**Lightly** spray a large flameproof casserole with the oil-water spray. Season the hake steaks with pepper and place in the casserole.

**Scatter** over the cleaned mussels and clams, then pour in the hot fish stock. Bring to the boil on a high heat, cover with a lid, reduce the heat and cook for 4–5 minutes until the fish is cooked and tender and the shellfish have opened.

**Remove** the fish and shellfish to 4 serving bowls.

**Return** the casserole to the heat and whisk in the 'butter', season to taste, then pour over the fish and serve.

**PER SERVING:**
200 KCALS, 5G FAT, 1G SATURATED FAT, 0.48G SODIUM

# bajan snapper

Marinating fish is one of the easiest ways to give it flavour, while the chilled dressing is the perfect foil for the spicy foods with which it is served. *Mojos* served all over the Caribbean islands with charcoal-grilled foods, such as fish and meats.

4 x 175g skinless, cleaned snapper fillets
4 spring onions
1 green pepper, deseeded and chopped
1 celery stick, chopped
1 red chilli, stem removed and chopped
1 tablespoon picked thyme leaves
1 tablespoon marjoram leaves
4 tablespoons chopped flat-leaf parsley
Juice of 2 limes

4 garlic cloves, peeled
Freshly ground black pepper
Oil-water spray (see page 33)

**For the mojo dressing**
1 mango, peeled and cut into 1cm dice
1 red onion, chopped
3 plum tomatoes, deseeded and cut into 1cm dice
1 garlic clove, crushed
Juice of 2 limes
2 tablespoons chopped mint
1 teaspoon caster sugar

**Serves 4**

**Preheat** the oven to 230°C/450°F/gas mark 8. To make the bajan paste, place the spring onions in a blender with the remaining ingredients except the snapper fillets and the oil and blitz to a paste.

**Place** the snapper fillet in a shallow dish and rub the paste all over both sides of the fish, cover with clingfilm and leave to marinate for a minimum of 2 hours at room temperature.

**To** make the mojo dressing, place all the ingredients in a bowl and marinate for 30 minutes. Remove any excess marinade from around the snapper fillets and place on a large non-stick baking tray, greased with a little oil-water spray. Place in the oven for 8–9 minutes until cooked.

**Dress** with the mojo dressing and serve on a bed of steamed white rice with some grilled pumpkin or squash.

**PER SERVING:**
250 KCALS, 3G FAT, 0G SATURATED FAT, 0.15G SODIUM

# pan-grilled tuna with swiss chard and moroccan salsa

To appreciate tuna at its best, it should be lightly cooked, otherwise it becomes dry.

1 tablespoon olive oil
½ teaspoon ground cumin
⅛ teaspoon ground turmeric
½ teaspoon ground cinnamon
2 roasted red peppers, peeled, deseeded and cut into 5mm dice
2 tomatoes, blanched, deseeded and cut into 5mm dice
12 black olives, pitted
100ml tomato juice
½ teaspoon cayenne

1 garlic clove, crushed
2 tablespoons roughly chopped coriander
2 tablespoons roughly chopped mint
75g fresh dates, stoned, peeled, cut into 5mm dice
Juice and zest of ½ orange
Juice of ½ lemon
Freshly ground black pepper
400g Swiss chard leaves
4 x 175g tuna fillet steaks

**Serves 4**

**Heat** half of the oil in a non-stick pan over a moderate heat, then add the cumin, turmeric and cinnamon and allow to infuse for 30 seconds. Add the red peppers, tomatoes, olives and tomato juice and cook for a further 2 minutes. Add the remaining ingredients, except the remaining oil, the chard and tuna. Season with black pepper to taste and keep warm.

**Cook** the chard for 2–3 minutes in a pan of boiling water, then remove and drain well. (Alternatively steam the chard in a colander over a pan of boiling water.)

**Heat** a ridged grill pan until it is almost smoking, then brush with the remaining oil. Season the tuna fillets and cook for 1–2 minutes on each side until charred on the outside, while the centre remains slightly pink.

**Dress** the chard with the tuna steaks, spoon the salsa over and serve. In keeping with the flavour of Morocco, fluffy steamed couscous would make an excellent accompaniment.

**PER SERVING:**
354 KCALS, 13G FAT, 3G SATURATED FAT, 0.51G SODIUM

# smoked chilli prawns with fennel and beetroot tzatziki

Tzatziki is a Greek salad made with cucumber and yogurt. Here I use beetroot, which has a sweet flavour to balance the yogurt. Also a wonderful colour, making a refreshing contrast for the spicy prawns.

1 large head fennel
100ml rice wine or white wine vinegar
3 tablespoons caster sugar
1 teaspoon smoked paprika
¼ teaspoon chilli powder
16 large tiger prawns, shelled and deveined
2 tablespoons chopped dill, plus whole leaves to garnish

4 lemon wedges, to garnish

**For the beetroot tzatziki**
100ml low-fat natural yogurt
2 medium beetroots, cooked and shredded
1 garlic clove, crushed
1 tablespoon red wine vinegar
1 tablespoon olive oil
Freshly ground black pepper

**Serves 4**

**Using** a kitchen mandolin set at its thinnest setting, slice the fennel, then place in a bowl. Heat the rice wine and sugar in a pan over a low heat until the sugar has dissolved. Pour the hot vinegar over the fennel, cover with clingfilm and set aside to marinate for 1 hour.

**In** another bowl, mix the paprika and chilli powder, then rub the prawns all over with the spice mix.

**To** make the tzatziki, mix the yogurt, beetroot and garlic in a bowl. Stir in the vinegar and olive oil, then season with black pepper.

**Heat** a non-stick frying pan and, when hot, dry-fry the prawns, turning them constantly until cooked and slightly charred all over; this should take about 2–3 minutes.

**Drain** the fennel and toss with the chopped dill. To serve, divide the fennel between 4 plates, top with some beetroot tzatziki, then the prawns. Garnish with the dill leaves and lemon wedges.

**PER SERVING:**
202 KCALS, 4G FAT, 1G SATURATED FAT, 0.29G SODIUM

# 'baked trout in the news'

The idea of cooking fish in newspaper came while on a trip to Scotland, salmon fishing for *The Sunday Telegraph* ten years ago. The gillie, John Burrow, showed us how to cook our catch on an open fire. Using the oven is fine for retaining the flavours.

2kg trout or salmon, gutted and
   scaled (ask your fishmonger to
   do this)
Freshly ground black pepper
60ml half-fat crème fraîche

4 sheets newspaper
1 sheet parchment paper
Oil-water spray (see page 33)
4 tablespoons dill
½ lemon, thinly sliced
60ml Pernod (or other
   anise-style liqueur)

**Serves 4**

**Preheat** the oven to 200°C/400°F/gas mark 6.

**Dry** the inside cavity of the trout with kitchen paper and season with black pepper. Place the newspaper and parchment paper under running water until they are wet.

**Lay** the newspaper sheets on top of each other on a flat surface, top with the wet sheet of parchment and spray with a little oil-water spray. Place the trout in the centre of the paper, pour over the crème fraîche and sprinkle liberally with the dill. Scatter the lemon slices over the fish, then pour over the Pernod.

**Carefully** wrap up the fish in the paper, tucking in the end to enclose the fish completely. Place on a baking sheet and bake in the oven for 30–40 minutes or until the wet paper is dry – an indicator that the fish is cooked.

**Unwrap** in front of your guests and cut into portions. Serve with courgettes, almonds and new potatoes.

PER SERVING:
373 KCALS, 13G FAT, 4G SATURATED FAT, 0.17G SODIUM

# miso ginger steamed salmon

I make no excuses for the strong Asian emphasis in this section of the book. I have a great love of this cuisine: delicate yet robust flavours that are low in fat, but high in taste. Miso paste can be bought from Oriental grocery stores or health-food stores.

1 tablespoon red miso paste
1 teaspoon unsaturated oil
2 tablespoons ketchap manis
   (Indonesian soy sauce)
5cm piece of root ginger,
   peeled and very finely chopped
1 tablespoon rice wine vinegar
1 tablespoon honey

4 x 175g fresh salmon fillets,
   skinned
2 small pak choi, halved
   lengthways
125g shiitake mushrooms,
   halved
6 spring onions, peeled and cut
   into 2.5cm lengths
Freshly ground black pepper

**Serves 4**

**In** a bowl, whisk the miso paste with the oil, half the soy sauce and the ginger. Pour in the rice wine vinegar and honey and stir well together.

**Place** the salmon fillets in a shallow dish, pour over the miso mixture and turn the fillets until well coated. Cover with clingfilm and place in the fridge for 1 hour.

**Remove** the salmon fillets from the marinade and wipe off any excess; discard the marinade. Place the fillets flat in a steamer basket, cover with the lid and place over a pan of boiling water. Cook for 3–4 minutes or until just tender.

**At** the same time, using another basket, steam the pak choi, mushrooms and spring onions for 3–4 minutes until cooked. Remove from the heat and season with black pepper. Serve the steamed vegetables topped with a steamed salmon fillet and drizzle around the remaining soy sauce.

PER SERVING:
354 KCALS, 20G FAT, 4G SATURATED FAT, 0.8G SODIUM

# salmon arrancini with tomato and cucumber dressing

Arrancini is the Italian term given to small orange-shaped balls made of rice with fish or meat, then deep-fried. Tinned salmon is ideal. Bake or grill with equally successful results.

200g risotto rice, cooked
1 free-range egg, hard-boiled and roughly chopped
200g tinned red salmon, drained and flaked
1 tablespoon chopped basil
1 tablespoon chopped parsley
Freshly ground black pepper
1 free-range egg white, beaten
150g fresh white breadcrumbs

1 lemon, sliced, to garnish
Green salad leaves, to garnish

**For the dressing**
100ml low-fat natural yogurt
2 tablespoons chopped basil
4 tomatoes, cut into 1cm cubes
100g cucumber, cut into 1cm cubes

**Serves 4**

**Place** the cooked rice in a bowl, add the egg, salmon and chopped herbs and season with black pepper. Place the mixture in the fridge for 1 hour to chill. Preheat the oven to 190°C/375°F/gas mark 5.

**Remove** the mixture from the fridge and shape into small balls about 4cm in diameter. Roll them through the beaten egg white, and then in the bread-crumbs, coating the balls evenly.

**Arrange** the arrancini on a non-stick baking sheet and place in the oven to cook for 10–25 minutes, until crisp and golden, or alternatively cook them under a hot grill, turning them occasionally.

**To** make the dressing, mix together the yogurt and basil, add the tomatoes and cucumber and season with black pepper. Drizzle the dressing over the arrancini and garnish with lemon and salad leaves. This dish is also great served with steamed new potatoes and green beans.

**PER SERVING:**
427 KCALS, 7G FAT, 1G SATURATED FAT, 0.52G SODIUM

# monkfish biryani

Monkfish is a very forgiving fish, and certainly responds well to forceful treatment. It is good for robust hearty dishes, combined with spices and herbs. Serve with yogurt and rice for a great meal.

350g basmati rice
2 teaspoons unsaturated oil
750g monkfish fillet, cleaned
1 onion, sliced
2.5cm piece of root ginger, finely chopped
2 garlic cloves, crushed
1 teaspoon ground coriander
½ teaspoon cumin seeds
1 teaspoon ground turmeric

½ teaspoon chilli powder
200g cauliflower, cut into florets
4 tomatoes, peeled and quartered
50g sultanas
1 teaspoon garam masala
2 free-range eggs, hard-boiled and quartered
75g cashew nuts
Coriander leaves, to garnish

**Serves 4**

**Place** the rice in a sieve and rinse under cold running water until the water runs clear, then put the rice in a saucepan with 600ml water. Bring to the boil, reduce the heat and simmer for 10 minutes or until the rice is tender. Drain well.

**Heat** 1 teaspoon of the oil in a heavy-based saucepan over a high heat. Add the monkfish fillet and seal for 1–2 minutes until golden all over, then set aside. Add the remaining oil, the onion, ginger and garlic and cook for 1 minute. Add the coriander, cumin, turmeric and chilli powder and fry for 2 minutes, stirring constantly to prevent the spices from catching on the pan and burning.

**Add** 600ml water to the spiced onion mixture and bring to the boil. Add the cauliflower, tomatoes and sultanas and simmer for 15 minutes. Add the rice, return the fish to the pan, stir in the garam masala and simmer for 2–3 minutes to allow the flavours to develop and finish cooking the fish. Serve garnished with the egg, cashew nuts and coriander.

**PER SERVING:**
665 KCALS, 16G FAT, 2G SATURATED FAT, 0.1G SODIUM

# chargrilled mackerel with tomato chutney and braised fennel

This chutney is a real winner, but is best made about 1 month in advance to allow the flavours to come through. Mackerel is full of good omega-3 fatty acids, hence the fat content of this recipe.

2 large heads of fennel, peeled
    and thickly sliced
Zest of ¼ lemon
300ml chicken stock (see page 39)
Freshly ground black pepper
1 tablespoon olive oil
1 garlic clove, crushed
Juice of ½ lemon
1 teaspoon smoked paprika
4 x 160g mackerel fillets

**Serves 4**

**For the tomato chutney**
150ml red wine vinegar
75g brown sugar
½ teaspoon dried chilli flakes
50g raisins
1 small onion, chopped
1 Granny Smith apple, peeled
    and chopped
400g tinned tomatoes,
    finely chopped
Pinch each of cayenne and
    ground cinnamon

**Preheat** the oven to 200°C/400°F/gas mark 6.

**To** make the chutney, place the vinegar, sugar, spices and raisins in a pan and bring to the boil, stirring until the sugar dissolves. Reduce the heat, add the onion, apple and tomatoes and simmer gently for 30 minutes until the mixture is thick. Season with cayenne and cinnamon and allow to cool.

**Place** the fennel on a roasting tray, add the lemon zest, pour over the stock and season with black pepper to taste. Cover with foil and bake in the oven until tender, this should take about 30 minutes.

**Place** the olive oil, garlic, lemon juice and smoked paprika in a dish, season the mackerel with black pepper and place in the marinade for 20 minutes.

**Grill** the fish on a barbecue or grill pan or under a hot grill until cooked and slightly charred. Serve the grilled mackerel on a bed of braised fennel with some tomato chutney.

**PER SERVING:**
535 KCALS, 29G FAT, 5G SATURATED FAT, 0.31G SODIUM

# mackerel tagine

Tagine is a staple of Moroccan cuisine and is traditionally cooked in an earthenware dish with a pointed lid. They are easy to prepare and are always flavourful and impressive.

Oil-water spray (see page 33)
1 onion, finely chopped
2 garlic cloves, crushed
¼ teaspoon fennel seeds
½ teaspoon ground cinnamon
¼ teaspoon smoked paprika
½ teaspoon dried chilli flakes
1 teaspoon ground cumin
½ teaspoon ground coriander
¼ teaspoon ground turmeric
1 small bay leaf
2 tablespoons sultanas

400g tinned tomatoes
1 teaspoon tomato purée
1 teaspoon harissa paste
    (hot spice paste)
450ml fish stock (see page 39)
425g tinned chickpeas,
    drained and rinsed
12 black olives, pitted
Freshly ground black pepper
700g mackerel fillets
Sprigs of fresh coriander,
    to garnish

**Serves 4**

**Heat** a non-stick frying pan with a little oil-water spray. Add the onion, garlic, fennel seeds and 2 tablespoons water, cover and sauté until the vegetables are soft, about 6–8 minutes.

**Add** all the spices, the bay leaf and sultanas and cook uncovered for 2–3 minutes to allow the spices to release their fragrance.

**Add** the tomatoes, tomato purée and harissa paste with the fish stock and bring to the boil. Cook over moderate heat until the sauce reduces and thickens in consistency. Add the chickpeas and olives.

**Season** with black pepper, then carefully lay the mackerel fillets on top. Cover with a lid and simmer over a gentle heat for 6–8 minutes or until the mackerel is cooked through. Dress the fish on to serving plates, pour over the sauce, sprinkle with the fresh coriander and serve.

**PER SERVING:**
539 KCALS, 32G FAT, 5G SATURATED FAT, 0.66G SODIUM

# linguine with anchovy olivada, tomatoes and capers

A pasta so simple to prepare, I am sometimes embarrassed to give the recipe, but oh, what flavour! Try it and see it for yourself. It can also be made with sardines.

1 teaspoon olive oil
2 shallots, finely chopped
1 garlic clove, crushed
8 salted anchovy fillets, rinsed, drained and finely chopped
8 black olives, pitted and finely chopped
100g sun-blush tomatoes, drained and roughly chopped
500g fresh or dried linguine pasta
1 tablespoon superfine capers, rinsed and drained
2 tablespoons roughly chopped flat-leaf parsley

**Serves 4**

**Heat** the oil in a non-stick pan, add the shallots and garlic and cook over low heat for 1 minute.

**Add** the anchovies, olives and tomatoes and heat gently over low heat.

**Cook** the pasta in plenty of boiling water until al dente, then drain, reserving 65ml of the pasta water.

**Add** the drained pasta and reserved water to the anchovy mixture, then add the capers and parsley. Toss well together and serve in deep pasta bowls.

PER SERVING:
496 KCALS, 5G FAT, 1G SATURATED FAT, 0.72G SODIUM

# baked smoked haddock pasta

Smoked haddock is a great fish, very flavourful and fairly inexpensive. Always buy natural smoked haddock rather than the yellow dried variety, which is more readily available. This is real comfort food, but without the calories.

4 rashers lean smoked bacon
310g bucatini pasta
200ml skimmed milk
350g smoked haddock fillet, skinned
1 free-range egg yolk
2 free-range egg whites
3 tablespoons half-fat crème fraîche
2 tablespoons half-fat Cheddar cheese
2 teaspoons Dijon mustard
Freshly ground black pepper

**Serves 4**

**Preheat** the oven to 190°C/375°F/gas mark 5. Place the bacon rashers on a non-stick baking tray and cook for 10 minutes until lightly crisp, remove and roughly chop into pieces. Cook the pasta in boiling water until al dente and drain well.

**In** a pan, bring the milk to the boil. Lower the heat, add the smoked haddock and poach for 3–4 minutes. Remove the fish with a slotted spoon and, when cool, lightly flake it, then strain the milk.

**Pour** the cooking milk into a bowl, and allow to cool slightly. Add the eggs, crème fraîche, half the Cheddar and the mustard, then season to taste with black pepper.

**Add** the fish and bacon to the cream mix and combine well together. Place the bucatini in an ovenproof baking dish, pour over the smoked haddock and bacon cream, toss together and scatter over the remaining Cheddar. Bake for 20–25 minutes until set and the top is bubbling and golden.

PER SERVING:
451 KCALS, 8G FAT, 3G SATURATED FAT, 1.32G SODIUM

# thai chicken bitoks

*Bitoks* are the name given to small burger-type patties. These bitoks may be prepared a day in advance, but if you do so, only top with the marinade for 2 hours before you want to serve. A simple but flavoursome dish, great for snacking as well.

450g lean chicken breasts, minced
2 free-range egg whites, lightly beaten
2 spring onions, chopped
1 tablespoon ketchap manis (Indonesian soy sauce)
2.5cm piece of root ginger, finely chopped
1 tablespoon chopped coriander
Freshly ground black pepper

**For the marinade**
2 tablespoons chopped coriander
1¼cm piece of root ginger, grated
1 garlic clove, crushed
½ teaspoon sweet chilli sauce
½ teaspoon ground turmeric
1 tablespoon peanut (groundnut) oil
1 tablespoon rice wine or white wine vinegar

**Serves 4**

**In** a bowl, combine the minced chicken with the egg whites, spring onions, soy sauce, ginger and coriander. Season with a little pepper and mix together. Using wet hands, mould into 8 small patties, about 2.5cm thick.

**Combine** all the marinade ingredients together with 1 tablespoon water in a bowl. Pour over the patties, cover with clingfilm and refrigerate for 2 hours.

**Remove** the patties from the marinade and place on a preheated grill pan or on a baking tray under a traditional preheated grill for 5–6 minutes, until cooked.

**Serve** with a traditional stir-fry of vegetables.

**PER SERVING:**
170 KCALS, 4G FAT, 1G SATURATED FAT, 0.37G SODIUM

# oriental sticky braised chicken

I love this chicken dish with its sweet-and-sour Oriental flavours. The chicken is marinated, then cooked until the sauce becomes thick and sticky.

4 large chicken legs, skin removed
5cm piece of root ginger, peeled, thinly sliced
90ml dry sherry
4 star anis
500ml chicken stock (see page 39)
100ml fresh or concentrated orange juice
1 tablespoon tamarind paste
3 tablespoons chopped Thai basil leaves

2 tablespoons roasted cashew nuts
Oil-water spray (see page 33)

**For the marinade**
2 lemongrass sticks, finely chopped
1 small red chilli, chopped
3 tablespoons ketchap manis (Indonesian soy sauce)
1 tablespoon honey

**Serves 4**

**To** make the marinade, mix all the ingredients together in a large bowl. Add the chicken legs, mix well with the marinade and leave for 2 hours at room temperature. Remove the chicken legs. Set aside the marinade.

**Squirt** a little oil-water spray in a non-stick frying pan and heat. Add the chicken legs and cook for 4–5 minutes until golden, then remove from the pan. Return the pan to the heat, add the ginger and sherry and boil for 2 minutes. Add the marinade and all the remaining ingredients except the Thai basil leaves, cashew nuts and chicken.

**Cook** over a high heat for 5–6 minutes, then return the chicken legs to the sauce. Cover with a lid and cook for a further 10 minutes until the sauce is reduced and sticky in consistency. Remove the star anis.

**Remove** the chicken legs to a serving dish and pour over the sauce. Sprinkle with the Thai basil and cashew nuts and serve with white rice and stir-fried vegetables.

**PER SERVING:**
310 KCALS, 7G FAT, 2G SATURATED FAT, 1.11G SODIUM

# cold chicken with tuna and blackbean corn salsa

This dish is based on the Italian dish *vitello tonnato*, poached veal set on a tuna sauce. Chicken makes a great and cheaper alternative, whilst the salsa gives the dish a little sparkle.

4 x 150g chicken breasts, skinless
150g tinned tuna in water, drained
1 tablespoon superfine capers, rinsed and drained
½ garlic clove, crushed
125ml reduced-calorie mayonnaise
Juice of ¼ lemon
Freshly ground black pepper
Handful of rocket leaves

**For the salsa**
75g dried black beans, soaked overnight
75g frozen sweetcorn kernels, defrosted
1 small red onion, chopped
½ garlic clove, crushed
Juice of ½ lemon
2 tablespoons maple syrup
1 tablespoon olive oil

**Serves 4**

**Steam** the chicken in a steamer over boiling water for 15–18 minutes, remove from the heat and allow to cool completely.

**To** make the salsa, drain the beans and place in a pan. Cover with water, bring to the boil and simmer for 30–40 minutes or until soft. Drain and cool. Place in a bowl, add the remaining ingredients and leave to infuse for 30 minutes.

**Place** the tuna, capers and garlic in a blender and blitz to a purée. Transfer to a bowl and stir in the mayonnaise and lemon juice. Season with black pepper to taste.

**To** serve, slice the chicken into 5mm thick slices. Divide the tuna sauce between 4 plates and top with the sliced chicken. Toss the rocket leaves in a little of the salsa juices and pile on the chicken.

**Spoon** over the salsa and serve with good crusty bread.

**PER SERVING:**
405 KCALS, 14G FAT, 3G SATURATED FAT, 0.52G SODIUM

# devilled chicken paillard with lemon and coriander couscous

Pomegranate molasses (also known as *dibs Rumen*) is a staple of the Middle Eastern countries. It is wonderfully sweet and syrupy, well worth sourcing from a Middle Eastern grocer.

4 x 175g chicken breasts, skinless
2 tablespoons wholegrain mustard
1 teaspoon Szechuan peppercorns, finely crushed
Juice and zest of ½ lemon
2 garlic cloves
1 tablespoon chopped oregano
1 tablespoon chopped coriander leaves
2 tablespoons pomegranate molasses
Oil-water spray (see page 33)

**For the couscous**
150g couscous
275ml hot chicken stock (see page 39)
75g currants, soaked in water and drained
2 tablespoons pine kernels
4 spring onions, shredded
4 tablespoons coriander leaves
Freshly ground black pepper

**Serves 4**

**Using** the side of a meat cleaver, lightly bash the chicken to obtain a thick steak-like breast of uniform thickness.

**In** a bowl, mix the mustard, Szechuan pepper, lemon juice and zest, garlic, herbs and molasses to form a light paste. Brush the chicken breasts all over with the paste and leave to marinate for 1 hour.

**Preheat** the grill to its highest setting.

**Place** the couscous in a large bowl, pour over the hot chicken stock, cover and leave to stand for 5–8 minutes. Fluff the couscous with a fork, then add the currants, pine kernels, spring onions and coriander, mix well and season with black pepper to taste.

**Lightly** spray a baking sheet with the oil-water spray. Place the chicken breasts on it and cook under the grill for 6-8 minutes until golden. Divide the couscous between 4 plates, place the chicken on top and serve.

**PER SERVING:**
402 KCALS, 7G FAT, 1G SATURATED FAT, 0.32G SODIUM

# Pollo arrabbiato (spicy chicken stew with pumpkin, chilli and tomatoes)

A spicy chicken dish I love to prepare, though I have to admit that I use a lot more chilli than in the recipe. *Arrabbiato* is the name of the spicy tomato sauce popular in Italy.

Oil-water spray (see page 33)
250g small pickling onions
2 tablespoons brown sugar
250g pumpkin, skin removed, cut into 2cm dice
2 garlic cloves, crushed
2 red chillies, deseeded and finely chopped
1.6kg chicken, cut into pieces, skin removed
Freshly ground black pepper
1 tablespoon balsamic vinegar
1 tablespoon oregano
100ml dry white wine
400g tinned tomatoes, chopped

**Serves 4**

**Preheat** the oven to 200°C/400°F/gas mark 6.

**Heat** a squirt of oil-water spray in a large flameproof casserole dish, then add the onions, cover and fry until golden, this should take about 10 minutes. Remove the lid, add the brown sugar and caramelise lightly. Add the pumpkin, garlic and chillies and cook for a further 5 minutes. Remove from the pan and set aside.

**Season** the chicken pieces with black pepper. Return the dish to the heat, add the chicken pieces and cook until they begin to colour, turning once or twice. Pour over the vinegar and cook for 1 minute. Return the vegetables to the pan, add the oregano and raise the heat. Pour over the wine, cook for 5 minutes, then add the chopped tomatoes. Season with black pepper, cover with a lid and place in the oven to cook for about 40–45 minutes or until the chicken is cooked and tender.

**Serve** with soft polenta.

PER SERVING:
310 KCALS, 5G FAT, 1G SATURATED FAT, 0.24G SODIUM

# posh coq au vin

A retro recipe based on a classic French dish, chicken in red wine is usually made with button mushrooms, but I've replaced them with the woody flavour of wild mushrooms. Dried wild mushrooms are now ready available, and need to be soaked before using.

Oil-water spray (see page 33)
4 large chicken legs, skinned and cut into thighs and drumsticks
1 tablespoon plain flour
Freshly ground black pepper
150g small pickling onions, peeled
4 bacon rashers, cut into strips
200g mixed fresh wild mushrooms, cleaned, sliced
2 garlic cloves, crushed
150ml good-quality red wine
1 tablespoon tomato purée
850ml hot chicken stock (see page 39)
2 sprigs of fresh thyme
1 small bay leaf

**Serves 4**

**Preheat** the oven to 200°C/400°F/gas mark 6. Heat a squirt of oil-water spray in a large non-stick flameproof casserole dish. Dust the chicken pieces with the flour mixed with black pepper. Add to the pan and fry for 4–5 minutes on each side until the chicken is browned. Remove the chicken from the pan and place to one side.

**Add** the onions and bacon and cook for 5 minutes, until browned all over. Then add the wild mushrooms and garlic and cook for a further 5 minutes until the mushrooms are browned. Add the red wine and boil for 2–3 minutes.

**Return** the chicken to the pan, add the tomato purée and carefully mix well. Add the stock a little at a time to form a sauce. Bring to the boil, tuck in the thyme and bay leaf, cover with a lid and place in the oven to cook for 25–30 minutes or until the chicken is tender and the sauce reduced in consistency and intense in flavour. Remove the thyme and bay leaf and serve with mashed potatoes and steamed spinach.

PER SERVING:
265 KCALS, 7G FAT, 2G SATURATED FAT, 0.89G SODIUM

# stuffed chicken with dried fruits, almonds and wild rice

An impressive chicken dish filled with wild rice. Wild rice is no relative of rice at all, but the grain of watergrass native to North America.

150g wild rice
4 x 175g chicken breasts, skinless
50g dried fruits, in 5mm dice
2 spring onions, finely chopped
25g nibbled almonds, toasted
25g raisins, soaked in water
   until swollen, drained
1 teaspoon smoked paprika
Freshly ground black pepper
2 tablespoons low-fat fromage frais
2 tablespoons coriander
2 teaspoons unsaturated oil

**For the corn and mustard salsa**
75g tinned sweetcorn
2 tomatoes, deseeded and
   chopped
1 tablespoon chopped
   coriander
Juice of 1 lime
1 teaspoon wholegrain mustard
1 tablespoon honey
1 garlic clove, crushed

**Serves 4**

**Steam** or boil the wild rice for 40–45 minutes until tender. To make the salsa, heat a non-stick frying pan. Drain the corn, then dry-fry until golden for 2–3 minutes, tossing it in the pan occasionally. Turn into a bowl, add the remaining ingredients and marinate for 1 hour.

**Preheat** the oven to 200°C/400°F/gas mark 6. Lay the chicken breasts on a work surface and, using a sharp knife, cut a pocket into them along the length of the sides, ensuring that you don't cut right through.

**Mix** together the rice, fruits, onions, almonds, raisins, paprika and pepper. Stir in the fromage frais and coriander, then mix well. Open the pocket of each chicken and fill with the rice stuffing. Close the pocket and secure with 2 cocktail sticks. Heat the oil in an ovenproof non-stick frying pan. Season the breasts with pepper and cook for 2 minutes over a moderate heat, until golden, turning to seal all over. Pour over 100ml water, cover and cook in the oven for 10–12 minutes or until the chicken is cooked, juicy and tender. Remove from the oven, coat with the corn salsa and serve.

PER SERVING:
456 KCALS, 8G FAT, 1G SATURATED FAT, 0.19G SODIUM

# stuffed chicken paupiettes with smoked ham and corn

I first saw cornflakes used as a coating for chicken when I worked in Dallas, America. It led me to think of endless possibilities, from stuffings to corn sauces. Here they make a coating for stuffed chicken rolls.

4 x 175g chicken breasts, skinless
100g low-fat soft cheese
1 garlic clove, crushed
2 tablespoons chopped
   flat-leaf parsley
100g smoked ham, diced
1 small tin sweetcorn, drained
1 free-range egg yolk
45g fresh white breadcrumbs

Good pinch of paprika
Oil-water spray (see page 33)

**For the coating**
75g cornflakes
30g fresh white breadcrumbs
30g flat-leaf parsley
2 tablespoons plain flour
1 free-range egg white,
   lightly beaten

**Serves 4**

**Preheat** the oven to 200°C/400°F/gas mark 6. Cut a slit down one side of each chicken breast, ensuring you don't cut right through.

**In** a bowl, combine the soft cheese, garlic, parsley, ham, corn, egg yolk and breadcrumbs. Carefully spoon the mixture into each chicken pocket, ensuring it is neat and compact.

**To** make the coating, place the cornflakes in a blender, add the breadcrumbs and parsley and blitz until the mix resembles fine crumbs. Transfer to a shallow dish. Carefully pass the chicken breasts though the flour, then the egg white, then finally pass through the crumbs.

**Place** the breasts on a non-stick baking sheet, squirt a little oil-water spray over each one, and bake in the oven for 20–25 minutes or until cooked.

**Serve** with leaf spinach and boiled new potatoes.

PER SERVING:
494 KCALS, 9G FAT, 4G SATURATED FAT, 0.99G SODIUM

# oven-steamed guinea fowl

Guinea fowl is a good low-fat option. It can be somewhat dry, but steaming it in a foil pouch keeps it moist and retains all the flavours.

4 x 150g guinea fowl breasts, skinless
1 tablespoon chopped coriander
1 tablespoon chopped marjoram
Juice of 1 lemon
1 tablespoon brown sugar

**Serves 4**

1 lemon, cut into 8 slices
12 asparagus spears
1 teaspoon Dijon mustard
2 tablespoons half-fat crème fraîche
100g black trompette wild mushrooms (or button mushrooms)
100ml vermouth

**Place** the breasts in a dish, sprinkle over the coriander, marjoram and lemon juice, scatter over the lime leaves and cover with clingfilm. Marinate for 2 hours in the fridge.

**Preheat** the oven to 200°C/400°F/gas mark 6. In a non-stick frying pan, heat the sugar with 65ml water and lightly caramelise. Add the lemon slices and caramelise on both sides. Set aside.

**Cook** the asparagus in boiling water for 2 minutes, remove with a slotted spoon, refresh in cold water and drain well. Combine the mustard and crème fraîche in a bowl, add the marinated breasts and mix well together.

**Take** 4 sheets of foil, each large enough to wrap a breast. Place a breast on each piece of foil, arrange some mushrooms and asparagus on top and douse with a little vermouth. Bring up the sides of the foil around the breasts and press the edges together to seal them. Place the pouches on a baking sheet and cook in the oven for 15–20 minutes.

**Remove** and transfer the pouches to 4 serving dishes. Allow your guests to open their own pouch at the table to experience the wonderful aromas within, and serve with boiled new potatoes and carrot purée.

PER SERVING:
244 KCALS, 6G FAT, 2G SATURATED FAT, 0.13G SODIUM

# baked poussin with chilli jam and yogurt

This chilli jam recipe is taken from my book *Raising the Heat*. It has many uses, not only as a dip or relish for Asian foods, but also, as I discovered, as a wonderful spicy topping for baked chicken.

4 x 450g poussins (baby chickens), with skin removed

**For the chilli jam**
100ml rice wine vinegar
75g soft brown sugar
75g raisins
2 shallots, finely chopped
1 garlic clove, crushed
200g red chillies, deseeded and chopped

½ tablespoon root ginger, chopped
1 teaspoon nam pla (fish sauce)
65ml low-fat natural yogurt
2 teaspoons chopped coriander
½ teaspoon ground turmeric
Freshly ground black pepper
Lime wedges and coriander, to garnish

**Serves 4**

**To** make the chilli jam, place the vinegar and sugar in a pan and bring to the boil slowly to dissolve the sugar. Add the raisins and cook to a light caramel; the liquid should be syrupy. Stir in the shallots, garlic, chillies, ginger and fish sauce, then remove from the heat and leave to cool. Place in a blender and blitz to a coarse purée. This can be made in advance and kept in the fridge for up to 4 weeks.

**Preheat** the oven to 200°C/400°F/gas mark 6. Using a small knife, cut slits into the breasts and legs of the poussins. In a bowl mix the chilli jam, yogurt, chopped coriander and turmeric, then rub it on to the chickens, ensuring it is rubbed into the slits in each bird.

**Place** the poussins into a large non-stick baking tin and cook in the oven for 25–30 minutes or until cooked, crisp and slightly charred all over. Serve garnished with lime wedges and coriander leaves.

PER SERVING:
353 KCALS, 4G FAT, 2G SATURATED FAT, 0.27G SODIUM

# turkey porchetta style with dried mustard fruits

Porchetta is a wonderful aromatic way of serving pork, Italian style, ideally suckling pig, but sometimes pork loin. This is a low-fat alternative using turkey breast, which works equally well.

4kg free-range turkey, skin and legs removed
1 tablespoon unsaturated oil
100ml dry white wine
600ml chicken stock (see page 39)

**For the mustard fruits**
150g caster sugar
150ml apple juice
310g ready-to-eat dried fruits (apricots, figs, prunes)
65ml white wine vinegar
2 tablespoons chopped candied lemon peel
1 teaspoon English mustard powder

**For the stuffing**
3 tablespoons chopped rosemary
2 tablespoons fennel seeds
8 garlic cloves, crushed
Juice and zest of 1 lemon
3 tablespoons chopped marjoram
2 bay leaves
1 tablespoon olive oil

**Serves 8**

**Preheat** the oven to 200°C/400°F/gas mark 6.

**To** make the stuffing, blitz together the ingredients to a coarse paste in a blender.

**Take** the breasts, reserving the legs for another use. Using a sharp knife, cut a slit in each breast lengthways about two thirds of the way along to form a pocket, ensuring that you do not cut right through.

**Using** a kitchen mallet or bat, open up the meat and lightly bat it out. Rub the stuffing paste all over the inside. Close the pockets and tie with kitchen string.

**Heat** the oil in a large non-stick baking tray on the hob and seal the turkey all over until golden. Remove from the hob and place the breasts on a wire rack set over a baking tin so that the fat can drip away. Place in the oven to roast for 50–60 minutes or until the juices run clear when the meat is pierced with a small knife. Be careful not to overcook as the meat will become dry.

**To** make the mustard fruits, combine the sugar, apple juice and 100ml water in a pan. Stir until the sugar is dissolved. Add the fruits and cook over a low heat for 20 minutes or until they are soft. Add the vinegar, stir and cook for a further 5 minutes, then add the candied lemon peel. Mix well, then stir in the mustard. Allow to cool to room temperature.

**When** the turkey is cooked, remove from the oven and keep warm. Put the baking tin on the hob, pour over the wine and boil for 2 minutes. Add the stock and boil until it is reduced by half. Remove any fat that may rise to the surface with a piece of kitchen paper.

**Cut** the turkey into slices, pour over the gravy and garnish with the mustard fruits. Serve with roasted butternut squash, broccoli and roasted new potatoes.

PER SERVING:
373 KCALS, 5G FAT, 1G SATURATED FAT, 0.2G SODIUM

# pheasant casserole with autumn fruits

Pheasant is traditionally roasted, but this game bird also makes a wonderful casserole, although chicken can easily be substituted. Pheasant is best during late autumn and winter – October and December.

1 oven-ready pheasant, cut into 8 pieces, skin removed
Freshly ground black pepper
2 tablespoons plain flour
1 tablespoon unsaturated oil
60ml calvados (apple brandy)
200ml apple juice
1 tablespoon honey

300g small pickling onions
750ml chicken stock (see page 39)
½ tablespoon Dijon mustard
2 celery sticks, thinly sliced
2 Granny Smith apples, peeled, cored and cut into wedges
1 pear, peeled, cored and cut into wedges
1 bay leaf

**Serves 4**

**Preheat** the oven to 180°C/350°F/gas mark 4.

**Place** the pheasant pieces in a bowl, season with pepper, sprinkle over the flour and mix well.

**Heat** the oil in a flameproof casserole. Pat the pheasant pieces with kitchen paper to remove any excess flour and place them in the pan. Cook over a moderate heat for 4–5 minutes or until browned.

**Pour** in the calvados and cook for 1 minute. Add the apple juice, honey and onions and cook until the mixture becomes slightly syrupy in consistency. Add the chicken stock and mustard and bring to the boil, then add the celery, apple and pear pieces and tuck in the bay leaf.

**Cover** with a lid and cook in the oven for 1–1½ hours or until tender. Discard the bay leaf and serve.

PER SERVING: 281 KCALS, 5G FAT, 1G SATURATED FAT, 0.36G SODIUM

# duck and parsnip pie

I first prepared this variation of a shepherd's pie on Carlton TV's *Food Daily*, some years ago with Mark Curry. It is full of flavour and duck makes a welcome change from the usual minced lamb.

1 tablespoon unsaturated oil
675g minced duck from 5 duck legs (remove the skin and all visible fat)
1 onion, finely chopped
1 carrot, cut into small dice
½ swede, cut into small dice
1 celery stick, cut into dice
1 garlic clove, crushed
1 tablespoon tomato purée
1 tablespoon plain flour

90ml hot chicken stock (see page 39)
200g tinned tomatoes
1 teaspoon chopped oregano
1 small bay leaf
1 teaspoon Dijon mustard
2 teaspoons Worcestershire sauce

**For the crust**
400g parsnips, cut into small chunks
200g potatoes, cut into chunks
300ml semi-skimmed milk

**Serves 4**

**To** make the crust. cook the parsnips and potatoes in boiling water for 20–25 minutes or until very tender. Drain. Mash, add the milk and beat to a smooth purée.

**Heat** the oil in a non-stick frying pan, then add the minced duck, a little at a time, and fry until sealed and golden. Remove to a colander and leave to drain to remove any excess fat.

**Return** the pan to the heat, add the vegetables and garlic and cook for 2–3 minutes. Return the meat to the pan, add the tomato purée and cook for 1 minute. Sprinkle over the flour and combine well. Gradually add the stock and tomatoes and stir until it forms a sauce. Add the herbs, mustard and Worcester-shire sauce, cover, reduce the heat and cook for 25 minutes.

**Preheat** the grill to its highest setting. Transfer the cooked duck mixture to a baking dish and top carefully with the mashed potatoes and parsnips. Grill until the topping is bubbly, golden and crispy. Allow to cool slightly before serving with cabbage or steamed carrots.

PER SERVING:
428 KCALS, 16G FAT, 4G SATURATED FAT, 0.4G SODIUM

# grilled balsamic venison steak with peppercorns and cranberries

Here are tender venison steaks in a hot and spicy, sweet sauce. Other game such as pheasant or partridge would work equally well, as would duck breast.

4 x 175g venison steaks,
   cut from the fillet
Freshly ground black pepper
½ teaspoon Chinese five spice
2 tablespoons balsamic vinegar
½ tablespoon honey
Oil-water spray (see page 33)
Flat-leaf parsley, to garnish

**Serves 4**

**For the sauce**
3 tablespoons cranberry jelly
1 tablespoon green
   peppercorns, drained,
   rinsed and dried
50g fresh or frozen cranberries
Juice and zest of 1 orange
90ml good-quality red wine
125ml beef stock
   (see page 39)
1 tablespoon balsamic vinegar

**Season** the venison steaks liberally with the black pepper, then rub in the five spice. Combine the vinegar and honey and brush liberally over the steaks. Set aside.

**In** a pan, heat all the sauce ingredients together and simmer gently for 10–15 minutes, or until the sauce is reduced and coats the back of a spoon.

**Heat** a grill pan until very hot and lightly spray with the oil-water spray. Add the venison steaks and cook over a high heat for 3–5 minutes for medium and pink, or leave them a little longer if you prefer them well done.

**Dress** the steaks on 4 serving plates and coat with sauce. Scatter over the parsley leaves and serve with puréed celeriac.

PER SERVING:
259 KCALS, 3G FAT, 0G SATURATED FAT, 0.14G SODIUM

# bulgogi barbecue pork

*Bulgogi* is a national dish of Korea and is traditionally stir-fried beef, marinated in soy sauce, with quite a strong, spicy flavour. This is my version – a great barbecue dish during the summer, but actually good at any time.

150ml reduced-salt soy sauce
75ml medium-dry sherry
2½cm piece of root ginger,
   peeled, finely shredded
2 garlic cloves, crushed

**Serves 4**

1 tablespoon sesame oil
½ teaspoon dried chilli flakes
1 tablespoon brown sugar
750g lean pork fillet, all fat
   removed
1 tablespoon lime juice
50g coriander leaves

**In** a pan, mix the soy sauce, sherry, ginger, garlic, sesame oil, chilli flakes and sugar, and gently bring to the boil.

**Place** the pork fillet in a shallow dish, then pour over the marinade. Cover and place in the fridge for a minimum of 4 hours, preferably overnight.

**Heat** a grill pan on the stove until very hot and almost smoking. Remove the pork fillets from the marinade and drain well. Reserve the marinade.

**Cook** the pork fillet on the hot grill for 10–12 minutes, turning it regularly during this time until it caramelises.

**Meanwhile,** bring to the boil the reserved marinade, add the lime juice and coriander and cook for 2 minutes.

**To** serve, slice the pork into 1cm slices and coat all over with sauce.

**Serve** with noodles or stir-fried rice.

PER SERVING: 319 KCALS, 10G FAT, 3G SATURATED FAT, 1.74G SODIUM

# sicilian-grilled lamb with saffron and raisin polenta

Believe it or not, this sauce is one I prepared for our staff dining room at the hotel. The staff loved it, I am glad to say. The saffron and raisins give the polenta a fragrant flavour.

1 teaspoon olive oil
2 garlic cloves, crushed
2 shallots, finely chopped
1 tablespoon sherry vinegar
2 teaspoons brown sugar
200g tinned tomatoes, chopped
12 best-quality black olives
65ml marsala wine
1 tablespoon superfine capers, drained and rinsed

4 x 175g lean leg of lamb steaks, fat removed
1 teaspoon oregano
2 tablespoons chopped basil

**For the polenta**
1 garlic clove, crushed
Good pinch of saffron
100ml skimmed milk
175g fine cornmeal (polenta)
50g raisins
2 tablespoons quark

Serves 4

**To** make the polenta, bring 750ml water to the boil in a pan with the garlic, saffron and milk. Carefully pour in the polenta and stir continuously to form a smooth consistency. Add the raisins, then reduce the heat and continue to cook over a low heat until the polenta thickens and its consistency resembles that of wet mashed potatoes, this should take about 20–25 minutes. Fold in the quark and keep warm.

**Heat** the olive oil in a pan, add the shallots and garlic and cook over a low heat until softened. Add the vinegar, sugar, tomatoes, olives and marsala and simmer for 10 minutes until reduced in thickness. Then add the capers and keep warm.

**Preheat** a grill pan and when smoking, add the steaks and sprinkle on the oregano and basil. Grill for 2–3 minutes on each side, a little longer if you prefer them more cooked.

**Serve** the polenta on 4 serving plates, top with the lamb, pour over a little sauce and serve.

**PER SERVING:** 517 KCALS, 17G FAT, 7G SATURATED FAT, 0.49G SODIUM

# aromatic lamb chops with ginger squash and coriander sambal

Wonderful for barbecues, this marinade with delicate Indian spices works well on chicken and pork too. Sambals often accompany rice or curry dishes in Indonesia and Malaysia.

1 onion, finely chopped
2 garlic cloves, crushed
1 red chilli, deseeded and finely chopped
1 teaspoon ground cumin
1 teaspoon ground cardamom
½ teaspoon ground turmeric
8 x 95g large, lean lamb cutlets

Serves 4

**For the squash**
2.5cm piece of fresh root ginger, finely chopped
4 tablespoons brown sugar
90ml balsamic vinegar
700g butternut squash, peeled
Oil-water spray (see page 33)

**For the coriander sambal**
50g coriander leaves
1 green chilli, deseeded and chopped
Juice of ½ lemon
½ small onion, chopped

**Preheat** the oven to 200°C/400°F/gas mark 6. In a bowl, combine the onion, garlic, chilli, cumin, cardamom and turmeric. Rub this mixture on to the cutlets, cover with clingfilm and leave to marinate for 4 hours at room temperature.

**In** a non-stick frying pan, gently heat the ginger, sugar and vinegar, until the sugar has dissolved.

**Cut** the squash into large wedges, place in a roasting tin and spray lightly with the oil-water spray. Place in the oven for 15 minutes until golden in colour. Add the ginger balsamic syrup, turn the squash in the syrup and continue cooking for a further 15 minutes.

**Spray** a grill pan with the oil-water spray and heat until very hot. Remove the cutlets from the marinade and cook in the pan for 3–4 minutes on each side until slightly charred.

**Meanwhile**, to make the sambal, place all the ingredients in a blender and blitz to a coarse texture. Dress the grilled cutlets on the squash and serve with a little sambal alongside.

**PER SERVING:** 375 KCALS, 13G FAT, 6G SATURATED FAT, 0.12G SODIUM

# honey-glazed gammon with chilli, plums and minted swede purée

I am a great lover of gammon steaks, although they can be salty. If so, soak them in a little milk for 1 hour prior to cooking. The swede purée is wonderful in this dish – a lovely accompaniment.

2 tablespoons honey
1 teaspoon Dijon mustard
1 tablespoon balsamic vinegar
4 thick gammon steaks, all
  visible fat removed
Oil-water spray (see page 33)

**For the swede purée**
1 large swede, cut into chunks

**Serves 4**

150ml semi-skimmed milk
2 tablespoons mint jelly

**For the plums**
6 large ripe plums, quartered
  and stoned
2 tablespoons caster sugar
1 red chilli, deseeded and
  finely chopped
2 tablespoons red wine vinegar
Juice of 1 lime

**To** make the purée, place the swede in a pan, cover with water and bring to the boil. Cook for 25 minutes or until very soft, then drain. Blend the swede and the milk to a smooth purée, then stir in the mint jelly until dissolved. Set aside, but keep warm.

**Mix** together the honey, mustard and vinegar, then brush liberally all over the gammon steaks. Heat a ridged grill pan and lightly squirt with the oil-water spray. Add the gammon steaks and grill for 3–4 minutes on each side until cooked.

**Place** the plums in a pan large enough so they can fit in one layer. In a small pan, dissolve the sugar with 65ml water. Add the chilli, heat gently and cook until the sugar caramelises to a rich golden colour. Remove from heat, add the vinegar and 100ml water and stir until well mixed. Pour over the plums and cook gently, basting the plums in the syrup as they cook. Add the lime juice and keep warm.

**To** serve, pile a mound of swede purée on each plate and top with a gammon steak and some spicy caramelised plums.

PER SERVING:
438 KCALS, 15G FAT, 5G SATURATED FAT, 3.45G SODIUM

# slow-braised beef with orange, cumin and olives

This dish comes from Morocco, where it is usually prepared with lamb or mutton. The intense flavours magnify during its long braising time.

700g lean chuck steak, all
  visible fat and sinew removed
1 onion, sliced
2 garlic cloves, crushed
2 carrots, sliced
Zest of 1 orange
2 sprigs of rosemary
300ml orange juice
  (fresh or concentrated)
2 tablespoons unsaturated oil

**Serves 4**

2 teaspoons ground cumin
400g tinned tomatoes,
  chopped
1 tablespoon tomato purée
700ml beef stock
  (see page 39)
12 best-quality black olives
1 tablespoon chopped mint
1 tablespoon chopped
  coriander leaves
40g flaked almonds, toasted

**A** day in advance, cut the meat into 5cm cubes and place in a large bowl. Add the onion, garlic, carrots, orange zest and rosemary. Pour over the orange juice, mix well, then cover and place in the refrigerator overnight.

**On** the day, preheat the oven to 200°C/400°F/gas mark 6. Drain off and reserve the excess liquid from the marinated meat, reserving the vegetables and herbs too. Dry the meat well with kitchen paper.

**Heat** a non-stick flameproof casserole until almost smoking, add the oil and fry the meat, a little at a time, until sealed and golden all over. Remove each batch from the pan and keep warm. To the same pan, add the drained vegetables and herbs from the marinade with the ground cumin and cook for 2 minutes. Add the tomatoes, tomato purée and reserved orange marinade juices. Add the stock and bring to the boil. Return the meat to the sauce, cover with a lid, then cook in the oven for 1–1½ hours or until the meat is tender.

**Remove** from the oven and stir in the olives and fresh herbs, then scatter over the almonds. Serve with pilaff rice and broccoli.

PER SERVING:
558 KCALS, 22G FAT, 4G SATURATED FAT, 0.65G SODIUM

# poached beef fillet with horseradish and caper sauce

We all tend to roast or grill beef, but poaching can be great as well as healthy. I do not suggest using a stock cube to make the broth for this dish. Ideally prepare your own, following the recipe on page 39.

850ml well-flavoured beef stock (see page 39)
1 sprig of thyme
1 small bay leaf
65ml dry sherry
4 x 175g beef fillet steaks
12 baby carrots
2 celery sticks, cut in 5cm lengths
12 baby leeks, trimmed

2 turnips, cut into wedges
8 heads of baby fennel

**For the sauce**
65ml low-fat natural yogurt
1 teaspoon grated horseradish
1 tablespoon superfine capers, drained, rinsed and chopped
2 tablespoons chopped parsley

**Serves 4**

**Heat** the beef stock with the thyme, bay leaf and sherry in a large high-sided pan. Bring to the boil, reduce the heat and simmer for 5 minutes.

**Heat** a non-stick frying pan and, when hot, dry-seal the beef fillets all over, then add to the stock. Cook for 8–10 minutes, then add the vegetables and cook for a further 5 minutes.

**Meanwhile**, to make the sauce, combine all the ingredients and mix well.

**Remove** the beef and cut into thick slices. Arrange in deep bowls, pour over the vegetables and stock and serve with the horseradish and caper sauce, boiled new potatoes and Savoy cabbage, if liked.

**PER SERVING:**
318 KCALS, 12G FAT, 5G SATURATED FAT, 0.5G SODIUM

# chargrilled fillet of beef with rocket salsa verde

This sensational dish looks and tastes delicious. Don't worry if fresh pumpkin is out of season, any seasonal squash variety will do. The salsa verde gives the beef a little bite.

450g pumpkin, peeled and cut into wedges
1 large head of fennel, cut into wedges
1 tablespoon chopped rosemary,
350ml chicken stock (see page 39)
4 x 150g lean fillet steaks, fat removed
Freshly ground black pepper
Basil leaves, to garnish

**Serves 4**

**For the rocket salsa verde**
50g rocket leaves
25g basil leaves
1 tablespoon chopped flat-leaf parsley
1 tablespoon capers, drained, rinsed and dried
1 garlic clove, crushed
1 tablespoon balsamic vinegar
1 teaspoon Dijon mustard
5 tablespoons hot water
1 level teaspoon olive oil
2 tinned anchovy fillets, drained and rinsed

**Put** the pumpkin, fennel and rosemary in a heavy-based saucepan. Pour in the chicken stock until it covers the pumpkin and boil. Cover and cook over a medium heat for 10–12 minutes. Remove the lid and reduce the heat to a simmer. Continue cooking for about 10 minutes until the vegetables are tender and syrupy. Check the vegetables while they are cooking, adding a little water if they stick to the pan.

**To** make the salsa verde, put all the ingredients in a blender and blitz until you have a coarse-textured, thick, green sauce.

**Season** the fillet steaks lightly with pepper and place them on a very hot preheated ridged cast-iron grill pan or barbecue grill. Cook until the steaks are seared and crusty underneath, then turn them over and cook the other side. Allow about 3–4 minutes each side for rare, 4–5 minutes for medium and 7–8 minutes for well done.

**Arrange** the pumpkin and fennel wedges on 4 serving plates. Place a fillet steak on top and drizzle over some salsa verde. Garnish with basil leaves and serve immediately.

**PER SERVING:** 261 KCALS, 11G FAT, 4G SATURATED FAT, 0.39G SODIUM

5

desserts

# drunken bananas and kumquats

A simple dessert with a lot of flavour, but no fat! Guests are always intrigued when their food arrives mysteriously wrapped in foil and there are always suitably appreciative noises when they open them and the aromas are released.

3 tablespoons apricot jam
2 tablespoons brown sugar
100ml dark rum
Juice and zest of 1 orange
1 vanilla pod
4 bananas
75g kumquats
Quark or low-fat fromage frais, to serve

**Serves 4**

**Preheat** oven to 200°C/400°F/gas mark 6.

**In** a pan, combine 100ml water with the apricot jam, sugar, rum, orange juice and zest and bring to the boil.

**Using** a small knife, carefully split the vanilla pod and scrape out the seeds into the pan.

**Peel** the bananas, but leave them whole. Halve the kumquats. Take 4 sheets of foil, approximately 25 x 15cm each and fold them into shallow boat-shaped pouches.

**Place** 1 banana and some kumquats in each piece, then pour over the apricot sauce. Fold up the sides of each pouch to seal it horizontally. Place on a large baking sheet and cook in the oven for 20 minutes.

**Take** to the table and allow the guests to open the parcels themselves. Serve with a generous spoonful of quark or low-fat fromage frais.

**PER SERVING:**
222 KCALS, 0G FAT, 0G SATURATED FAT, 0.01G SODIUM

# baked fruit kebabs on chocolate couscous

You may be surprised to see sweet couscous used as a base for these fruit kebabs, but you'll soon discover that the chocolate works really well and makes an interesting variation.

2 oranges
2 bananas
1 ripe pear
4 pitted prunes, soaked and halved
4 tablespoons sugar
2 tablespoons rum (optional)

**For the couscous**
200ml skimmed milk
1 teaspoon ground cinnamon
40g sugar
½ tablespoon cocoa powder
100g couscous
90ml rum (optional)

**Serves 4**

**For** the couscous, heat the milk, cinnamon and sugar in a small saucepan, add the cocoa, stir well and bring to the boil. Place the couscous in a bowl, pour over the chocolate milk, stir well, then cover and leave to stand for 5–8 minutes.

**Separate** the grains of couscous with a fork, cover and leave for a further 5 minutes. Stir once again, add the rum, if using, and leave in the fridge.

**Soak** four bamboo skewers in cold water, for about 30 minutes. Preheat the oven to 230°C/450°F/gas mark 8.

**Peel** the oranges, bananas and pear. Cut each banana into 8 thick slices and cut the oranges into quarters. Halve the pear, remove the core, then cut into quarters.

**Thread** the fruit on to the skewers, with the prune halves at each end of the skewers. Place the fruit skewers in a shallow ovenproof dish. In a pan, boil the sugar with 4 tablespoons water for 5 minutes to make a syrup. Pour over the skewers, leaving a little aside for basting, and douse with rum, if using. Bake in the oven for 5 minutes, basting occasionally with syrup.

**Serve** the chilled couscous topped with the fruit kebabs, pouring over any remaining syrup.

**PER SERVING:**
304 KCALS, 1G FAT, 0G SATURATED FAT, 0.05G SODIUM

# chocolate and banana gratin

Here's a dish with a flavour that is reminiscent of my childhood when I used to eat banana splits. Bananas baked with rich chocolate – delicious. This gratin has been created on the same lines and is very simple to make.

3 large free-range egg yolks
100ml condensed skimmed milk
100ml skimmed milk
3 tablespoons chocolate milk shake flavouring
1 large banana
4 teaspoons caster sugar

**Serves 4**

**Preheat** the oven to 150°C/300°F/gas mark 2. Whisk the egg yolks together with both milks and the chocolate flavouring until creamy. Strain through a fine sieve into a bowl.

**Divide** the mixture into 4 small ramekins. Place in a roasting tin, then fill the roasting tin with hot water until the water reaches halfway up the sides of the ramekins.

**Cook** in the oven for 45–50 minutes, remove from the oven and cool. If you like, you can keep the custards in the fridge once cooled, until needed.

**To** serve, peel the banana and cut into thick slices. Arrange slices on top of the custards so that they overlap.

**Sprinkle** the caster sugar evenly over the bananas, then place under a preheated grill until golden and caramelised, or use a kitchen blowtorch.

**Allow** to cool slightly before serving.

**PER SERVING:**
228 KCALS, 5G FAT, 1G SATURATED FAT, 0.06G SODIUM

# strawberry romanoff

A great dessert during the summer when strawberries are at their best. There are French, Russian and American versions of this dish and a true Romanoff will also include a liqueur.

150g packet of strawberry jelly
200g strawberries, cut into pieces
150ml fat-free milk powder
4 tablespoons half-fat crème fraîche
2 tablespoons roughly chopped mint, plus whole mint leaves to garnish

**For the biscuits**
60g reduced-fat spread
100g caster sugar
2 free-range egg whites
6 tablespoons plain flour, sifted
Oil-water spray (see page 33)

**Serves 4**

**To** make the romanoff, prepare the jelly following the instructions on the packet. Allow to cool to just warm.

**Place** 75g of the strawberries in a blender, blitz to a purée and set aside.

**Mix** the milk powder into the warm jelly and, using a hand blender, whip the jelly until it becomes airy in texture. Fill 4 tumbler-style glasses with the jelly mixture until they are three-quarters full, then place in the refrigerator to set. Mix the remaining strawberries with the crème fraîche and chopped mint.

**Preheat** the oven to 190°C/375°F/gas mark 5. To make the biscuits, beat the spread, sugar and egg whites in a bowl with an electric mixer until pale in colour. Stir in the flour. Lightly grease a baking tray with a squirt of oil-water spray. Place the mixture in a piping bag and, using a 1cm tube, pipe eight 8cm lengths on the baking tray. Bake for 5–6 minutes or until the edges are brown and the biscuits cooked. Allow to cool before serving.

**To** serve, remove the Romanoff from the fridge, top with the crème fraîche and strawberries, pour over the strawberry purée and garnish with the biscuits and whole mint leaves.

**PER SERVING:**
504 KCALS, 9G FAT, 3G SATURATED FAT, 0.39G SODIUM

# pears in port and cranberry syrup

The colours in this dish are amazing: scarlet red pears in a contrasting syrup. A dish that is sure to impress and ideal for autumn and winter entertaining when pears are at their best.

4 large firm but ripe pears (William, Comice)
300ml cranberry juice
100ml port
100g caster sugar
Zest of 1 orange
½ cinnamon stick
200g fresh or frozen cranberries
Sprigs of mint, to garnish
Buttermilk and lemon sorbet (see page 154), to serve

**Serves 4**

**Using** a potato peeler, peel the pears neatly, leaving the stalks intact and retaining the shape of the fruit. Cut a little off the base of each pear to help it remain upright during poaching. Choose a saucepan that will hold the 4 pears upright side by side. Place the cranberry juice, port, sugar, orange zest and cinnamon in the pan and bring to the boil, stirring, until the sugar has dissolved. Add the pears, cover the pan and simmer for 20–25 minutes or until the pears are tender when pierced with a knife, but still retaining their shape.

**Using** a slotted spoon, remove the pears from the syrup and leave to cool. Add the cranberries to the syrup and boil rapidly until reduced by two thirds. Allow to cool, then pour the syrup and cranberries over the pears and place in the fridge for up to 4 hours to chill thoroughly.

**Garnish** with mint and serve with the Buttermilk and Lemon Sorbet, although low-fat vanilla yogurt would make a good alternative.

PER SERVING:
233 KCALS, 0G FAT, 0G SATURATED FAT, 0.02G SODIUM

# coffee marsala nectarines with crème fraîche

For me coffee and Marsala are natural flavour partners. They instill a sweet yet bitter flavour that works so well. This is an elegant, sophisticated dish, perfect for a dinner party.

8 ripe but firm nectarines
100g caster sugar
1 tablespoon Camp coffee essence
1 vanilla pod, split in two
1 cinnamon stick
65ml Marsala wine
100ml half-fat crème fraîche, to serve

**Serves 4**

**Preheat** the oven to 180°C/350°F/gas mark 4.

**Blanch** the nectarines in boiling water for 1 minute, remove and refresh quickly in cold water. Remove and peel the skins. Halve the nectarines, remove the stones and place the fruit in a baking tin.

**Boil** 300ml water with the sugar, cook for 10 minutes to form a light syrup. Add the coffee essence, vanilla, cinnamon and Marsala wine. Pour over the nectarines and bake, uncovered, for 25 minutes until the nectarines are cooked, basting regularly.

**Remove** the spices and vanilla from the syrup.

**Using** a slotted spoon, remove the fruit to a dish and allow to cool. Pour the remaining syrup into a pan and reduce over a high heat by one third of its volume. Pour over the nectarines and allow to cool completely. Chill overnight in the syrup and serve with crème fraîche.

PER SERVING:
255 KCALS, 4G FAT, 2G SATURATED FAT, 0.04G SODIUM

# apple and cherry baklava with cinnamon syrup

Baklava is a speciality of Greece and the Middle East. Normally the filo pastry is full of crunchy nuts, baked and then drizzled with warm syrup; here I have come up with an apple and cherry variation.

2 Granny Smith apples
50g raisins
30g caster sugar
150g cherries, stoned
50g walnut halves, chopped
50g almonds, chopped
1 teaspoon ground cinnamon
1/8 teaspoon ground cloves
75g fresh brioche crumbs
 (or breadcrumbs)

3 filo pastry sheets
2 free-range egg whites, lightly beaten
Low-fat fromage frais or half-fat crème fraîche, to serve

**For the syrup**
100g caster sugar
Zest and juice of 1/2 lemon
25ml honey
1/2 teaspoon ground cinnamon

Serves 4

**Preheat** the oven to 200°C/400°F/gas mark 6. Peel the apples, remove the cores and cut into large chunks. Place in a pan with the raisins, sugar and 4 tablespoons water. Cover and cook over a medium heat for 8–10 minutes, until the apples are soft but not mushy and no liquid remains. Set aside to cool.

**When** cooled, add the cherries, nuts, spices and crumbs and bind the whole mix together well. Lay one sheet of filo on a flat surface, brush with egg white. Top with second sheet, brush, then top with the last sheet, brushing again with egg white. Cut the filo to form 4 squares. Divide the apple and cherry mix between the 4 squares, then bring up the sides of each to form a pouch and scrunch the top to seal in the apple filling. Brush over each pouch with egg white, then place on a baking sheet and bake for 12–15 minutes until golden.

**Meanwhile**, prepare the syrup. Place the sugar with 100ml water in a pan and stir over a low heat until dissolved. Add the lemon zest and juice, honey and cinnamon, then boil for 6–8 minutes. Remove from the heat and allow to cool. Spoon the syrup over the baklava and serve.

PER SERVING:
554 KCALS, 17G FAT, 2G SATURATED FAT, 0.39G SODIUM

# gingernut bread pudding

Ever since my working days at London's Dorchester Hotel under chef Anton Mosimann, I have loved the bread and butter pudding we prepared lovingly to this recipe. I have created lots of variations on it over the years, well here's another.

2 tablespoons maple syrup
10 slices of white bread, crusts removed
100g ready-to-eat dried figs
100g ready-to-eat dried apricots
75g gingernut biscuits, crushed
50g flaked almonds, toasted

Serves 4

750ml skimmed milk
2 large free-range eggs
40g caster sugar
1 vanilla pod, split, seeds removed
65ml amaretto (almond liqueur; optional)
65ml reduced-sugar apricot jam, warmed
Icing sugar for dusting

**Preheat** the oven to 150°C/300°F/gas mark 2.

**Brush** the maple syrup over the bread slices, then cut the bread into large cubes and place in a bowl. Add the dried fruits, gingernut biscuits and toasted almonds. Scatter the bread and fruit evenly over the base of a 1.2 litre ovenproof dish.

**In** a bowl, whisk together the milk, eggs, sugar, vanilla and amaretto liqueur, if using. Pour the milk mixture over the fruit and bread, ensuring all the bread is immersed in the milk.

**In** the oven, heat a large roasting tin containing enough water to come halfway up the sides of the ovenproof dish.

**Place** the ovenproof dish in the roasting-tin water and bake the pudding in the oven for 45–50 minutes until the top is lightly golden and it is just set. Remove and allow to cool slightly, then brush all over with the warmed apricot jam. Dust with icing sugar and serve warm.

PER SERVING:
619 KCALS, 16G FAT, 3G SATURATED FAT, 0.72G SODIUM

# cherimisu

This dish is my humorous take on tiramisu, the classic Italian dessert, but without mascarpone, and this variation will soon become a favourite in your home. Leaf gelatine can be hard to find, so, as a guide, a 25g packet of powdered gelatine equals 4 leaves.

65ml kahlúa (coffee-flavoured liqueur)
45ml maraschino (cherry liqueur)
50g brown sugar
50g caster sugar
3 gelatine leaves
450ml low-fat soft cheese or quark
Zest of ½ orange
Zest of ½ lemon
12 boudoir biscuits (or sponge fingers)
65ml Camp coffee essence mixed with 90ml boiling water
400g tinned morello cherries in syrup, well drained
2 teaspoons cocoa powder, for dusting

**Serves 4**

**Warm** the liqueurs together in a pan with the sugars, until hot. Add the gelatine leaves and stir well until dissolved. Set aside to cool.

**In** a bowl, combine the cheese with the lemon and orange zest, and stir in the liqueur mix.

**Soak** the boudoir biscuits in the coffee essence for 3–4 minutes, then arrange a layer of fingers in a serving dish, followed by a layer of cheese mix. Scatter over some drained cherries and repeat the layers until the ingredients are used up.

**Dust** the top with the cocoa powder, and chill for up to 4 hours before serving.

**PER SERVING:**
387 KCALS, 2G FAT, 1G SATURATED FAT, 0.12G SODIUM

# caramelised pineapple and strawberries with anis and saffron syrup

I go through phases when I use a particular ingredient regularly. Star anis is one favourite that I am using at present in dishes from desserts to sauces and sorbets.

65ml dry white wine
100g caster sugar
5cm piece of orange peel
3 star anis
1 vanilla pod
Pinch of saffron
2 tablespoons Pernod (or other anise-style liqueur)
4 slices of fresh pineapple
200g strawberries, halved

**Serves 4**

**Place** 100ml water in a pan with the wine and 65g of the sugar and bring to the boil slowly to dissolve the sugar.

**Add** the orange peel, star anis, vanilla pod and saffron, simmer gently for 15–20 minutes until the syrup has thickened slightly, then strain through a sieve.

**In** a non-stick pan, heat the remaining sugar and the Pernod and caramelise lightly. Add the pineapple and strawberries and caramelise in the sugar. Pour over the syrup and cook for 2 minutes.

**Serve** warm, with low-fat vanilla ice cream.

**PER SERVING:** 173 KCALS, 0G FAT, 0G SATURATED FAT, 0.01G SODIUM

# not-so-humble black crumble

I truly believe that some of the best desserts in the world originate in the UK. In fact, during my travels, I have seen many chefs trying to recreate British favourites, such as the legendary apple crumble. Here is one I concocted with a low-fat regime in mind.

50g caster sugar
150g firm ripe plums, halved
200g black figs, quartered
125g blackberries
150g blueberries

**For the topping**
75g plain flour
1 tablespoon cocoa powder
½ teaspoon ground cinnamon
25g brown sugar
50g low-fat spread
75g amaretti biscuits, finely crushed

Serves 4

**Preheat** the oven to 200°C/400°F/gas mark 6.

**To** make the topping, place the flour, cocoa powder, cinnamon, sugar and low-fat spread in a bowl. Mix well, then add the amaretti biscuits.

**In** a pan, add the sugar to 100ml water and heat until it forms a light syrup. Add the plums and poach for 5 minutes, then remove from the heat and add the remaining fruits.

**Place** the fruits in a 600ml ovenproof dish. Sprinkle over the crumble topping and bake in the oven for 15–20 minutes until golden and crispy.

**Serve** with low-fat fromage frais or low-fat custard, if liked.

PER SERVING:
325 KCALS, 8G FAT, 2G SATURATED FAT, 0.22G SODIUM

# peanut butter cheesecake tart

In this cheesecake recipe, the biscuit forms a coating on the top of the tart rather than on the base. If you can't find leaf gelatine, see the note in the introduction to Cherimisu on page 150 for the powdered gelatine equivalent.

150g smooth peanut butter
350g low-fat soft cheese or quark
Zest of 1 orange
40ml rum
50g caster sugar
100ml semi-skimmed milk

Serves 8

4 gelatine leaves, soaked in cold
    water until soft, then drained
2 free-range egg whites
1 x 20cm prepared sweet
    pastry tart case

**For the topping**
50g sweet digestive biscuits
2 tablespoons honey

**In** a blender, combine the peanut butter, cheese, orange zest, rum and sugar, blitz until smooth, then transfer to a bowl. Heat the milk until hot, then add the soaked gelatine. Allow to cool, then stir into the cheese mix.

**Beat** the egg whites until stiff peaks form and fold into the mixture. Pour into the prepared tart case and level off to a smooth surface. Place in the fridge to set overnight.

**Preheat** the oven to 180°C/350°F/gas mark 4.

**To** make the topping, crush the biscuits coarsely and mix with the honey. Place on a baking sheet and cook for 15–20 minutes until the biscuits and honey slightly caramelise. Allow to cool, then blitz in a blender until they resemble fine crumbs.

**Dust** the cheesecake tart with the crumbs and serve with a low-fat ice cream.

PER SERVING:
353 KCALS, 19G FAT, 5G SATURATED FAT, 0.26G SODIUM

# low-fat sorbets

Here are a few of my favourite low-fat sorbets based on simple ingredients. They are easy to prepare, but work best when you use a sorbet machine. There are some reasonably priced machines on the market now, and they are well worth the investment. **Serves 4**

## raspberry and vodka sorbet

375g fresh or frozen raspberries, defrosted if frozen
65ml vodka
375g caster sugar

**Place** the raspberries and vodka in a blender and blitz until smooth, then strain through a fine sieve.

**Put** the sugar and 370ml water in a pan, slowly bring to the boil, then reduce the heat and simmer for 10 minutes or until the mixture becomes a thick syrup. Allow to cool, add the raspberries and vodka and mix well. Place in a sorbet or ice-cream machine and freeze according to the manufacturer's instructions.

PER SERVING:
429 KCALS, 0G FAT, 0G SATURATED FAT, 0.01G SODIUM

## passion fruit and lime sorbet

375g caster sugar
Juice of 2 limes
375g fresh passion fruit pulp and seeds

**Put** the sugar and 370ml water in a pan, slowly bring to the boil, then reduce the heat and simmer for 10 minutes or until the mixture becomes a thick syrup.

**Allow** to cool, add the lime juice and passion fruit and mix well. Place in a sorbet or ice-cream machine and freeze according to the manufacturer's instructions.

PER SERVING:
404 KCALS, 0G FAT, 0G SATURATED FAT, 0.02G SODIUM

## buttermilk and lemon sorbet

250g caster sugar
500ml buttermilk
Juice and zest of 1 lemon
1 tablespoon honey

**Put** the sugar and 250ml water in a pan. Slowly bring to the boil, then remove from the heat. Pour into a bowl and chill in the fridge for 1 hour.

**In** a bowl, whisk together the buttermilk, lemon juice and zest and honey. Slowly add the syrup. Place in a sorbet or ice-cream machine and freeze according to the manufacturer's instructions.

PER SERVING:
304 KCALS, 1G FAT, 0G SATURATED FAT, 0.08G SODIUM

## ricotta sorbet

250g caster sugar
600g ricotta cheese
2 tablespoons honey

**Put** the sugar and 250ml water in a pan. Slowly bring to the boil, then remove from the heat. Pour into a bowl and chill in the fridge for 1 hour.

**Place** the ricotta and honey in a food processor and slowly blend in the chilled syrup. Place in a sorbet or ice-cream machine and freeze according to the manufacturer's instructions.

PER SERVING:
502 KCALS, 18G FAT, 11G SATURATED FAT, 0.17G SODIUM

# layered summer pudding

One of Britain's greatest desserts, a real treat at any time. A friend's wife gave me the idea of using a fruit jelly instead of gelatine to bind it. It really is simple and easy to prepare, and my version is layered rather than moulded.

750g mixed summer fruits (e.g. blackcurrants,
    redcurrants, strawberries, raspberries)
100g caster sugar
2 tablespoons crème de cassis (blackcurrant liqueur – optional)
1 packet raspberry or strawberry jelly
½ loaf sliced white bread, crusts removed

**Serves 8**

**Remove** the stalks from the currants. Trim the tops from the strawberries, then cut the strawberries in half.

**Place** all the fruits except the raspberries in a pan with the sugar and add 350ml water and the cassis liqueur, if using. Simmer gently for 5 minutes, then add the raspberries and cook for a further 2 minutes.

**Remove** from the heat and drain the fruits from the liquid. Set aside the fruits and return the liquid to the boil. Stir in the jelly and remove from the heat. Stir until all the jelly has dissolved. Allow to cool, then chill in the fridge for 10 minutes or until the jelly starts to thicken but not set. Remove the jelly from the fridge and mix the chilled jelly with the fruits again.

**Cut** the bread slices in half and place a layer on the base of a small gratin dish, with the slices overlapping. Place some of the fruits over the bread and level off. Top with a second layer of bread, then more fruits, finishing with a layer of bread. Push down the bread to ensure it is immersed in the juices, cover the dish with foil and place in the fridge for up to 4 hours to set.

**To** serve, cut out sections of the pudding and serve with a low-fat cream or ice-cream.

**PER SERVING:**
161 KCALS, 0G FAT, 0G SATURATED FAT, 0.11G SODIUM

# index

# resources

**UK**
**British Heart Foundation**
Greater London House
180 Hampstead Road
London
NW1 7AW
020 7554 0000
Heart Helpline:
0300 330 3311 (Mon-Fri 9am-6pm)
www.bhf.org.uk

**HEART UK**
7 North Road
Maidenhead
Berkshire
SL6 1PE
0845 450 5988
www.heartuk.org.uk

**British Dietetic Association**
Charles House, Great Charles Street
Queensway
Birmingham
West Midlands
B3 3HT
0121 200 8080
www.bda.uk.com

**US**
**American Heart Association**
National Center
7272 Greenville Avenue
Dallas
TX 75231
1-800-AHA-USA-1 (1-800-242-8721)
www.americanheart.org

**CANADA**
**Heart and Stroke Foundation of Canada**
222 Queen Street, Suite 1402
Ottawa
ON K1P 5V9
(613) 569-4361
www.heartandstroke.ca

**AUSTRALIA**
**National Heart Foundation of Australia**
Cnr Denison St & Geils Court
Deakin
ACT 2600
1300 36 27 87
www.heartfoundation.org.au

**Heart Support Australia**
PO Box 266
Mawson
ACT 2607
0262 852357
www.heartnet.org.au

**Acknowledgements**
With special thanks to the following people who have made this book possible: to Linda Tubby for her inspired food styling and to Pete Cassidy for the magnificent photographs. Penny Markham for the props, Lara King for her patience and good nature with recipe typing and Carl Hodson for his design. Not forgetting Kyle and project editor Muna Reyal for all her support, always being at the end of the telephone for me, when I needed her and most of all for her encouragement. PG